I0842021

ENTREPRENEURSHIP

IN LIBRARIANSHIP

VIVIEN OLUCHI EMMANUEL

ENTREPRENEURSHIP IN LIBRARIANSHIP

© Copyright 2023 Vivien Oluchi Emmanuel

ISBN: 9798863367934

Published in Nigeria by:

Nkanemi Services

nkanemiservices@gmail.com

All rights reserved. No portion of this book may be reproduced, stored in a retrieval system, or transmitted in any form or by any means without the prior written permission of the author except for brief quotations in critical reviews or articles.

TABLE OF CONTENTS

Business Plan

ACKNOWLEDGEMENT

First and foremost, I sincerely thank God Almighty who has been my greatest source of inspiration. He has taken me beyond my expectation and I know that he will continue to spur me on. May his name be praised in Jesus Name Amen.

I sincerely thank my lovely husband for his encouragement and support. I also thank my outstanding children for always praying for me. God bless you for allowing me thise exclusive moments to brainstorm.

My indebtedness goes to Prof. Okee Okoro for given me a professional touch to this work. I really appreciate your efforts SIR Also, I am grateful to my HOD Prof. Blessing Ahiauzu for her mentorship, Prof Nonyelum Okpowasili, Dr. Innocent Ordu for going through some chapters of this book and to all members of LIS family, Rivers State University Port Harcourt.

No one author can claim to have produced something substantial without consulting related materials, I therefore thank all the authors whose works are cited in this book. I also thank who did the typesetting, formatting and design of this book, God bless you all.

DEDICATION

This book is dedicated to my **OUTSTANDINGS:** Fortune, Favour, Destiny and Divine Emmanuel, thank you my honeypies for always praying "Father Lord help my mummy to make her own book" God has indeed answered your prayers from your innocent Hearts.

CHAPTER ONE

AN OVERVIEW OF ENTREPRENEURSHIP

The world is crazy about innovations and new products that entrepreneurs can offer in the market. To this end, Graduates of library and information science (GLIS) have to showcase their acquired skills and knowledge and not to worry about being thrown into the labour market. No matter how crowded the market may look, it should not bother them because it is not for them. This is because, librarians are "food basket of the universe" as mother of knowledge, if librarians refuse to sell their products which are information based, the world will suffer from information malnutrition. Librarians should therefore look inward (out of box) and release all their products for the consumption of the general public.

In this information age, the roles of information as the fourth economic resource cannot be overemphasis. Information is a marketable commodity and a social wealth. According to Ugwu and Ezeani, (2012), Technological innovations and new ideas are borne out of information sourcing, processing and dissemination thereby empowering and creating wealth for the library and information professionals

In response to markets, product obsolescence, customers' needs, new technologies or a combination of these factors in the business world, firms sometimes change their primary products or services. In pursuit of higher returns on investment, companies often change business directions in order to thrive. Contemporarily, any firm that is unwilling to change its course in terms of products and services to meet changing needs of its clients is bound to face consequences such as bankruptcy.

The perception that technology has changed the way most organizations conduct their services and operations has led to the push to be entrepreneurial. The implication is that librarians could also do business as well as utilize market strategies in advertising its products and services.

Though it is often not evident to the general public, library vendors are beginning to diversify their products and services as well. According to Hutchinson (2019), Libraries have responded to their own "customers" by beginning to provide services that had previously been outside their range. He went further to state that, some public libraries now circulate materials like board games, cookware, toys and tools besides books and media. According to him, other libraries, including those in the academic world, now contain non-collections areas such as maker spaces that may include 3D printers and other digital tools. These services may be in demand, but they are largely outside the traditionally defined realm of libraries as collections of print materials.

Because traditional library vendors have often collected and managed publishing data, their new services include tools to measure and evaluate citations and other research metrics, as well as other products that provide comparisons of research activity, collaborations and outputs. These products tend to be targeted at research administration, not libraries. Likewise, many commercial publishers have developed and now sell or support tools for scholars as authors rather than readers.

All of these mean that librarians are increasingly encouraged to be entrepreneurial. Although many librarians work in a not-for-profit setting, academic librarians are not immune to the influence of business, sales, markets and other commercial forces. The scholars who use research libraries may be isolated from these factors by their labs, courses or field work, but librarians cannot avoid dealing with the products, vendors and discounts that ultimately affect them. Certainly, with regard to scholarly communication services and the regular journal cancellation exercises that many libraries undertake, librarians have been forced to think about the business models of publishers and vendors (and even library operations) like never before. (Davis, 2015).

Adaptation to user preferences is happening in libraries. The new services that libraries offer to their clients have defined them from traditional collection-building and reference activities that they were known for. Online access has made life easier and as a result, users visit the physical library less often. Librarians are now encouraged to explore services in various areas such as

Scholarly communication consultation, Xeroxing, publishing, data management and, all of which may require a more entrepreneurial approach.

Who is an Entrepreneur?

Economists have never had a consistent definition of "entrepreneur" or "entrepreneurship" (the word "entrepreneur" comes from the French verb *entreprendre*, meaning "to undertake"). Though the concept of an entrepreneur existed and was known for centuries, the classical and neoclassical economists left entrepreneurs out of their formal models: They assumed that perfect information would be known to fully rational actors, leaving no room for risk-taking or discovery. It was not until the middle of the 20th century that economists seriously attempted to incorporate entrepreneurship into their models.

Three thinkers were central to the inclusion of entrepreneurs: Joseph Schumpeter, Frank Knight, and Israel Kirzner. Schumpeter suggested that entrepreneurs—not just companies—were responsible for the creation of new things in the search of profit. Knight focused on entrepreneurs as the bearers of uncertainty and believed they were responsible for risk premiums in financial markets.

Other definitions of entrepreneur are stated below:

An entrepreneur is an individual who creates a new business, bearing most of the risks and enjoying most of the rewards. The entrepreneur is commonly seen as an innovator, a source of new ideas, goods, services, and business/or procedures. In a nutshell, an entrepreneur is:

- A person who identifies business opportunities that will fill gaps in the market

- A person who undertakes the risk of starting a new business venture.
- A person who creates a firm, which aggregates capital and labour in order to produce goods or services for profit.
- One who is an important driver of economic growth and innovation.
- Resilient (all entrepreneurs have failures and successes history. Hence,

  an entrepreneur has the ability to learn from mistakes and move on with the business).

Figure 1: Summary Definitions of an Entrepreneur

1725: Richard Cantillion:	An entrepreneur is a person who pays a certain price for a product to resell it at an uncertain price, thereby making decisions about obtaining and using the resources while consequently admitting the risk of enterprise.
1803: J.B. Say	An entrepreneur is an economic agent who unites all means of production - land of one, the labour of another and the capital of yet another and thus produces a product. By selling the product in the market he pays rent of land, wages to labour, interest on capital and what remains is his profit. He shifts economic resources out of an area of lower and into an area of higher.
1845: Jean-Baptiste Say	An entrepreneur is an organizer whose input gives value to the other resources when combined in the production process.
1934: Schumpeter	An entrepreneur is an innovator who uses a process of shattering the status quo of the existing products and services, to set up new products and new services.
1961: David McClleland	An entrepreneur is a person with a high need for achievement [N -Ach], He is energetic and a moderate risk taker
1964: Peter Drucker	An entrepreneur searches for change, responds to it and exploits opportunities. Innovation is a specific tool of an entrepreneur hence an effective
1971: Kilby	An entrepreneur is an imitator who does not innovate but imitates technologies innovated by others. These are very important in developing economies.

1975: Albert Shapero	Entrepreneurs take initiative, accept risk of failure and have an internal locus of control.
1983: G. Pinchot	An entrepreneur is an Intrapreneur within an already established organization
1983, 1985; Stevenson, 1991, Stevenson and Jarillo:	An entrepreneur is one who pursues opportunities beyond the resources currently
1993: Baumol	An entrepreneur is an innovator, someone who transforms innovations and ideas into economically viable entities; independent of whether in the process she creates or
2013: Ronald May	An Entrepreneur is someone who commercializes his or her innovation.

Adapted from Robert (1986).

Going by the above definitions and discussions, it can be understood that there is, no "one-best definition" of the term entrepreneurship, all the scholars taking from their different point of view still make sense.

To an economist, an entrepreneur is one who brings resources, labour, materials and other assets into combinations that make their value greater than before, and also one who introduces changes, innovations, and a new order. Entrepreneurship involves certain factors such as risk taking, competition, wealth creation, time, among others.

We can therefore sum it up with Akinola (2013) who sees entrepreneurs as 'ice breakers', innovators and visionaries who see opportunities in obtrusive challenges.

The skills and characteristics of an entrepreneur

An entrepreneur is someone with the foresight, drive and ambition to take a risk and solve business or consumer problems. Some of the key characteristics a successful entrepreneur requires include:

1. Passion
2. Innovative
3. Persistent – doesn't take no for an answer

4. Resourceful
5. Risk-taker
6. Discipline

Passion for your business

For one to succeed in any giving profession or skill there must be a passion for that particular job. Having Flair for a thing goes a long way in bringing out the best in someone. To some people, pure passion and drive is the single most defining characteristic of a successful entrepreneur. Someone that has a passion for a thing focuses all his energies into turning his concept into a profitable reality.

It is that passion which helps an entrepreneur to identify business opportunities where others cannot and even if others do see the same opportunity and competition arises, their passion for what they do means competition never scares them rather, it merely spur them on to do better.

Innovation

An entrepreneur is always on the look-out for new innovations and ways of reinventing themselves. Whether those innovations come from within or from outside sources, they seek inspiration to find better ways to run their businesses and refine the products and services they offer. Apart from their innovative nature, successful entrepreneurs are not rigid they are flexible to accept and adopt change when necessary for the growth of their business. They may be persistent, but they are not too pig-headed to fail to acknowledge when new methods can outperform existing ones.

Perseverance in turning their business dream into a reality

No- giving-up is a good entrepreneurial spirit, there's a clear difference between *thinking* about a business idea and *pursuing* a business idea and making it work. Those with the inquisitive nature and perseverance to follow ideas and aspirations through are considered to have the entrepreneurial spirit and good sense.

Resourceful: from one-man-band to thriving company

Generally, resources are limited in nature and for that reason, a key ingredient for any entrepreneur that wants to be successful in business is to maximise the resources at hand. As a one-man-band, entrepreneurs need to be able to manage their time with supreme efficiency and also have the foresight to seek help when they need it.

Resourceful entrepreneurs create a network of people they can trust and tap into when they are looking for a specialist task completed.

At the early stages of any business, the purse strings are usually as tight as they will ever be. You need to be able to learn to survive as a business before you can thrive. The ability to find out what works before scaling it up by launching a minimum viable product or service is a major trait of any successful entrepreneur.

Prepared to take a risk

An entrepreneur needs to be Comfortable and always ready to take risks after identifying a potential opportunity by investing time, resources and effort into it to make it a success. Very often, these risks will be well-calculated, weighing up the potential benefits of taking a risk. In many cases, not taking risks can suppress a new business before it even gets off the ground!

As calculated risk-takers, entrepreneurs need to be careful with their financial planning; and not too conceited to ask for professional financial and legal advice when they need it most. This is to say that in order for entrepreneurs to make sound business decisions, they need access to a wide range of reliable and relevant information and advice

Entrepreneurs Impact the Economy

To economist, an entrepreneur acts as a coordinating agent in a capitalist economy. This coordination takes the form of resources being diverted toward new potential profit opportunities. The entrepreneur moves various resources, both tangible and intangible, promoting capital formation.

In a market full of uncertainty, it is the entrepreneur who can actually help clear up uncertainty, as he makes judgments or assumes the risk. To the extent that capitalism is a dynamic profit-and-loss system, entrepreneurs drive efficient discovery and consistently reveal knowledge. Established firms face increased competition and challenges from entrepreneurs, which often spurs them toward research and development efforts as well. In technical economic terms, the entrepreneur disrupts course toward steady-state equilibrium.

Entrepreneurs Help Economies

Nurturing entrepreneurship can have a positive impact on an economy and the society in several ways. For starters, entrepreneurs create new business. They invent goods and services, resulting in employment, and often create a ripple effect, resulting in more and more development.

Entrepreneurs add to the gross national income. Existing businesses may remain confined to their markets and eventually hit an income ceiling. But new products or technologies create new markets and new wealth. An increased employment and higher earnings contribute to a nation's tax base, enabling greater government spending on public projects.

Entrepreneurs create social change. They break tradition with unique inventions that reduce dependence on existing methods and systems, sometimes rendering them obsolete. Smartphone and their apps, for example, have revolutionized work and play across the globe.

How Entrepreneurs Work

Entrepreneurship is one of the resources economists categorize as essential to production, the other three being land, labour and capital. An entrepreneur combines the first three of these to manufacture goods or provide services. They typically create a business plan, hire labour, acquire resources and finances, hence provide leadership and management for the business. Entrepreneurs commonly face many obstacles when building their companies.

The three that many of them cite as the most challenging are: overcoming bureaucracy, hiring talent and obtaining financing.

The Entrepreneur and Finance

Considering the risk involvement in starting up a new venture, the acquisition of capital funding is particularly challenging, and many entrepreneurs deal with it via bootstrapping: financing a business using methods such as using their own money, providing sweat equity to reduce labour costs, minimizing inventory, and factoring receivables. While some entrepreneurs are lone rangers struggling to get small businesses off the ground on a shoestring, others take on partners armed with greater access to capital and other resources. In these situations, new firms may acquire financing from venture capitalists, angel investors, hedge funds, crowd-sourcing, or through more traditional sources such as bank loans.

What is Entrepreneurship?

Several scholars have defined entrepreneurship in different ways, but there appears to be no universally acceptable definition of the term. Everyone seems to have his or her own views about what it is and as such have defined it. Therefore, whatever definition one comes up with depends on the perspective one looks at it from. The term entrepreneurship is therefore a multidimensional concept.

Kirzner thought of entrepreneurship as a process that leads to discovery. Davis (2015) sees entrepreneurship as the creation and running of one's own business. While Shane and Venkataraman (2000) emphasize that it is a "nexus" that involves entrepreneurial individuals seizing and exploiting lucrative opportunities: "the field involves the study of sources of opportunities; the processes of discovery, evaluation, and exploitation of opportunities; and the set of individuals who discover, evaluate, and exploit them".

Enikanselu (2008) argues that entrepreneurship has to do with people that have the ability to see and move forwards business opportunity, gather the necessary resources benefit from them and to initiate appropriate action to ensure success. Entrepreneurship empowers people, in all societies and at all levels, to take their own destiny into their hands. It creates opportunities which not only contribute to economic growth, but also to personal and professional development.

According to Drucker (1985), entrepreneurship is defined as 'a systematic innovation, which consists in the purposeful and organised search for changes, and it is the systematic analysis of the opportunities, such changes might offer for economic and social innovation.'

United Nations Industrial Development Organisation (UNIDO) (1999) defined entrepreneurship as the process of using initiative to transform business concept to new venture, diversify existing venture or enterprise to high growing venture potentials. Kuratko and Hodgetts (2007) develop an integrated definition that acknowledges the critical factors needed for the entrepreneurship. They concluded that:

Entrepreneurship is a dynamic process of vision, change, and creation.

It requires anapplication of energy and passion towards the creation and implementation of new ideas and creative solutions. Essential ingredients include the willingness to take calculated risks—in terms of time, equity, or career; the ability to formulate an effective venture team; the creative skill to marshal the needed resources; the fundamental skill of building a solid business plan; and, finally, the vision to recognise opportunity where others see chaos, contradiction, and confusion.

According to Nwachukwu (2009) Entrepreneurship is the purposeful activity of an individual or group of associated individuals, under-taken to initiate, maintain, or aggrandise a profit-oriented business unit for the production or distribution of economic goods and services.

Entrepreneurship sometimes is being substituted with other words such as:

enterprise, innovation, small business, growth companies, etc. To fully capture and understand the entrepreneurship phenomenon, it is important to know the meanings of some of these entrepreneurial related words like: Entrepreneur-Individual Entrepreneurial Process, Entrepreneurial- Attitudes, skills and behaviours and Entrepreneurial ecosystem, a role of society.

Entrepreneur-Individual

Entrepreneurship is consequent upon individuals. There is normally - differentiation between individual entrepreneurs or businessmen (independent) and corporate entrepreneurs or businessmen associated with the higher echelons of a firm's management when referring to entrepreneurs. Different names have been used to describe the latter such as "corporate entrepreneurship", "corporate venturing", "entreprencurship", "interne corporate entrepreneurship" and "strategic renewal". The individual entrepreneur detects or creates business opportunities that he or she then exploits through micro, small and medium-sized firms. Participating in funding the capital for that firm, the entrepreneur carries out the role of arbitrator or simply "sells the idea" of the business project. The "corporate entrepreneur" or the chief executive of large firms must also be considered. This figure is no longer limited to efficiently managing the firm's assets, coordinating and controlling its activities; in the current climate, he or she must anticipate, articulate and manage change.

Entrepreneurial Process:

Entrepreneurship is a process, a progression, a development, a journey, to a destination which is profitable; a means, not an end. All the successful entrepreneurs went through a process. Entrepreneurs are change agents in that they integrate various factors of production to provide something new and novel to the community by means of their innovative and creative ideas.

Entrepreneurial Ecosystems

There is research that shows high levels of self-employment can stall economic development: Entrepreneurship, if not properly regulated, can lead to unfair market practices and corruption, and too many entrepreneurs can create income inequalities in the society. Overall, though, entrepreneurship is a critical driver of innovation and economic growth. Therefore, fostering entrepreneurship is an important part of the economic growth strategies of many local and national governments around the world.

To this end, governments commonly assist in the development of entrepreneurial ecosystems, which may include entrepreneurs themselves, government-sponsored programs and venture capitalists. They may also include non-government organizations, such as entrepreneurs' associations, business incubators, and education programs.

Road to Entrepreneurship

Unlike traditional professions, where there is often a defined path to follow, the road to entrepreneurship is baffling to most. What works for one entrepreneur might not work for the next and vice versa. That said, there are five general steps that most, if not all, successful entrepreneurs have followed:

1. Ensure Financial Stability
This first step is not a strict requirement but is definitely recommended. While entrepreneurs have built successful businesses while being less than financially flush (think of Facebook founder Mark Zuckerberg as a college student), starting out with an adequate cash supply and ensuring ongoing

funding can only help an aspiring entrepreneur, increasing his or her personal runway and give him more time to work on building a successful business, rather than worrying about making quick money.

2. Build a Diverse Skill Set

Once a person has strong finances, it is important to build a diverse set of skills and then apply those skills in the real world. The beauty of step two is that, it can be done concurrently with step one.

Building a skill set can be achieved through learning and trying new tasks in real-world settings. For example, if an aspiring entrepreneur has a background in finance, he can move into a sales role at his existing company to learn the soft skills necessary to be successful. Once a diverse skill set is built, it gives an entrepreneur a toolkit that he can rely on when he is faced with the inevitability of tough situations.

3. Consume Content across Multiple Channels

As important as building a diverse skill set is, the need to consume a diverse array of content is equally so. This content can be in the form of podcasts, books, articles or lectures. The important thing is that the content, no matter the channel, should be varied in what it covers. An aspiring entrepreneur should always familiarize himself with the world around him so he can look at industries with a fresh perspective, giving him the ability to build a business around a specific sector.

4. Identify a Problem to Solve

Through the consumption of content across multiple channels, an aspiring entrepreneur is able to identify various problems to solve. One business adage dictates that a company's product or service needs to solve a specific pain point—either for another business or for a consumer group. Through the identification of a problem, an aspiring entrepreneur is able to build a business around solving that problem.

It is important to combine steps three and four by so doing, it becomes possible to identify a problem to solve by looking at various industries as an outsider. This often provides an aspiring entrepreneur with the ability to see a problem others might not.

5. Solve That Problem

Successful start-ups solve a specific pain point for other companies or for the public. This is known as "adding value within the problem." Only through adding value to a specific problem or pain point does an entrepreneur become successful.

Entrepreneurs play a key role in any economy, using the skills and initiative necessary to anticipate needs and bring high-quality new ideas to market. Entrepreneurs who prove to be successful in taking on the risks of a start-up are rewarded with profits, fame, and continued growth opportunities. Those who fail suffer losses and become less prevalent in the markets.

Shrewd Money Management

Through the heart of any successful new business, venture beats the lifeblood of steady cash flow—essential for purchasing inventory, paying rent, maintaining equipment and promoting the business. The key to staying in the black is rigorous bookkeeping of income versus expenses. And since most new businesses don't make profit within the first year, by setting money aside for this contingency, entrepreneurs can help mitigate the risk of falling short of funds. Related to this, it's essential to keep personal and business costs separate, and never dip into business funds to cover the costs of daily living.

Of course, it is important to pay yourself a realistic salary that allows you to cover essentials, but not much more—especially where investors are involved. Similarly, such sacrifices can strain relationships with loved ones who may need to adjust to lower standards of living and endure worry over risking family assets. For this reason, entrepreneurs should communicate these issues well ahead of time, and make sure significant loved ones are spiritually on board.

Questions for Entrepreneurs
Embarking on the entrepreneurial career path to "being your own boss" is exciting. But along with all your research, make sure you do your homework about yourself and your situation.

A Few Questions to Ask Yourself:

- Do I have the personality, temperament, and mindset of taking on the world on my own terms?

- Do I have the required ambiance and resources to devote all my time to my venture?
- Do I have an exit plan ready with a clearly defined timeline in case my venture does not work?
- Do I have a concrete plan for next "x" number of months or will I face challenges midway due to family, financial or other commitments? Do I have a mitigation plan for those challenges?
- Do I have the required network to seek help and advice as needed?
- Have I identified and built bridges with experienced mentors to learn from their expertise?
- Have I prepared the rough draft of a complete risk assessment, including dependencies on external factors?
- Have I realistically assessed the potential of my offering and how it will figure in the existing market?
- If my offering is going to replace an existing product in the market, how will my competitors react?
- To keep my offering secure, will it make sense to get a patent? Do I have the capacity to wait that long?
- Have I identified my target customer base for the initial phase? Do I have scalability plans ready for larger markets?
- Have I identified sales and distribution channels?

Questions That Delve into External Factors:

- Does my entrepreneurial venture meet local regulations and laws? If not feasible locally, can I and should I relocate to another region?
- How long does it take to get the necessary license or permissions from concerned authorities? Can I survive that long?
- Do I have a plan about getting the necessary resources and skilled employees, and have I made cost considerations for the same?
- What are the tentative timelines for bringing the first prototype to market or for services to be operational?
- Who are my primary customers?
- Who are the funding sources I may need to approach to make this big? Is my venture good enough to convince potential stakeholders?
- What technical infrastructure do I need?
- Once the business is established, will I have sufficient funds to get resources and take it to the next level? Will other big firms copy my model and kill my operation?

Correct answers to above Factors, will help an intending entrepreneur to be armed with necessary tools for a successful entrepreneurial activities.

Intrapreneur

The concept "intrapreneurship" is beginning to spread rapidly in modern times. The word 'intrapreneur' was introduced by Gordon Pinchot and officially recognised in 1992. According to Kenton (2020), The term intrapreneurship refers to a system that allows an employee to act like an entrepreneur within a company or other organization. Intrapreneurs are self-motivated, proactive, and action-oriented people who take the initiative to pursue an innovative product or service. While American Heritage Dictionary defined intrapreneurship as "A person within a large corporation who takes direct responsibility for turning an idea into a profitable finished product through aggressive risk-taking and innovation." "Intrapreneurs are people working within corporations who approach their work in an entrepreneurial fashion," This involves entrepreneurship inventiveness and spirit within an organisation rather than outside. It provides opportunities to hard-to-find key employees of an organisation to unfold their potentials, performance and hard work to earn a reward or share in the profit or revenue generated by his inventiveness for the enterprise (Nwosu, 2014).

An intrapreneur has the knowledge that failure does not cost him anything as it does to an entrepreneur since the organization bears all losses that may arise from failure. This is because the company furnishes the Intrapreneurs with every necessary resources required for operations while entrepreneurs provide for themselves all needed resources. In a nutshell it should be noted that:

- Intrapreneurship is a system which allows an employee to act like an entrepreneur within an organization.
- Intrapreneurs are self-motivated, proactive, and action-oriented people who have leadership skills and think outside the box.
- Intrapreneurship is one step toward entrepreneurship—intrepreneurs can use what they have learned as part of a team to develop their own businesses.

Understanding Intrapreneurships
An intrapreneurship creates an entrepreneurial setting by allowing employees to use their entrepreneurial skills for the benefit of both the company and the employee. This gives employees the liberty to explore, as well as the opportunity to grow within an organization.

Intrapreneurships promote self-sufficiency and autonomy, while trying to find the best decision. For example, an intrapreneurship may require an employee to research and recommend a more efficient workflow chart to a company's brand within a target group or implement a way to benefit company culture.

It's important for employers to identify these workers. It can be very detrimental to a brand or company if an employer of labour fails to promote intrapreneurship or recognize employees who demonstrate an intrapreneurial spirit. Employers who encourage intrapreneurship stand to benefit because it leads to the success of the department or the company as a whole. Keeping these employees can help lead to innovation and growth. Companies that don't promote them may lose such intrapreneurs to other companies, or they may end up working for themselves.

Locating intrapreneurs sometimes can be tricky but no matter how difficult, it is worth doing because, these employees are generally self-starters who are both pushy and goal oriented. They are often able to solve problems on their own, and come up with ideas that lead to process improvements. An intrapreneur may also take certain risks by assuming multiple responsibilities even some that he or she may not be comfortable with all in search of new challenges.

Characteristics of Intrapreneurs
A thriving intrapreneur is comfy being uncomfortable while trying his or her ideas until achieving the looked-for results. Intrapreneurs are able to resolve

specific issues such as growing output or cutting expenses and this requires a high level of skill—namely leadership skills and thinking outside the box—directly pertinent to the obligation. He or she is also able to understand trends in the marketplace and envisage how the company needs to go forward to stay ahead of its competition. The intrapreneur is part of a company's backbone and the motivating force mapping out the organization's prospect. An intrapreneur also takes risks and drives novelty within a business to better serve the market through improved goods and services (Kenton, 2020)

Distinction between Entrepreneurship and Intrapreneurship:

An entrepreneur is someone who, through his or her skills and passion, creates a business and is willing to take full accountability for its success or failure. An intrapreneur, on the other hand, is someone who utilizes his or her skill, passion and innovation to manage or create something useful for someone else's business... with entrepreneurial zest.

Intrapreneurs vs. Entrepreneurs

- Entrepreneurs provide the spark. Intrapreneurs keep the flamegoing.

- Entrepreneurs are found anywhere their vision takes them. Intrapreneurs work within the confines of an organisation.

- Entrepreneurs face many hurdles, and are sometimes ridiculed and riddled with setbacks. Intrapreneurs may sometimes have to deal with conflict within the organisation.

- Entrepreneurs may find it difficult to get resources. Intrapreneurs have their resources readily available to them.

- Entrepreneurs may lose everything when they fail. Intrapreneurs still have a paycheque to look forward to (at least for now) if they fail.

- Entrepreneurs know the business on a macro scale. Intrapreneurs are highly skilled and specialised.

What makes entrepreneurs and intrapreneur similar is the passion to see things through to the end and the courage to face failure.

Note Worthy

It is note worthy that intrapreneurship is one step toward entrepreneurship. Intrapreneurs can develop and use their creativity to enhance existing goods and services within the context of the business, all without any of the risk attached to being an entrepreneur. Intrapreneurs may use what they've learned as part of an organization's team to create their own company and reap the benefits of their hard work rather than letting another organization profit from their ideas.

CHAPTER TWO

THEORIES OF ENTREPRENEURSHIP

A theory is a contemplative and rational type of abstract or generalizing thinking about a phenomenon, or the results of such thinking. The process of contemplative and rational thinking often is associated with such processes like observational study and research. It can also be said to be a set of interrelated concepts, definitions, and propositions that explains or predicts events or situations by specifying relations among variables. Wikipedia May 5, 2014

In other words, it can be said to be a deduction or a system of ideas intended to explain something, chiefly one that based on general philosophy independent of the thing to be explained.

Theory is important because, it provides concepts to name what we observe and to explain relationships between them. It gives room for one to put in plain words what he observed and to figure out how to bring about change. Theory is a tool that enables one to identify a problem and also a means for savaging the situation. Furthermore, theory functions majorly in describing, explaining, and predicting behaviour. It stimulates and guides the further development of knowledge. In general, theory is concerned with the systematic description and explanation of a particular phenomenon.
Many scholars over the years have made contributions to the theory of entrepreneurial development and many more are still propounding new theories on the same subject. Entrepreneurship theory therefore remains important to the development of the entrepreneurial field.

This chapter examines some entrepreneurship theories with underlying empirical studies.

These are (1) Discovery theory, (2) Creation Theory (1) Economic entrepreneurship theory, (3) Psychological entrepreneurship theory (4) Sociological entrepreneurship theory, (5) Anthropological entrepreneurship theory (6) Opportunity-Based entrepreneurship theory, (7) Resource-Based entrepreneurship theory etc. These theories offer us a fairly good opportunity to refocus our efforts at integrating the diverse viewpoints.

There are different theories of entrepreneurship; some of them are as follows:

1. **Discovery Theory**

It includes Individual/Opportunity (I/O) nexus view, which lays emphasis on the identification, existence, and exploitation of opportunities and their influence on individuals. The individuals and the opportunities have influence on each other. For example, an opportunity comes into existence only when an individual identifies it, simultaneously an individual takes up the entrepreneurial activity because of the existing opportunity.

This theory approaches three assumptions in entrepreneurship, which are as follows:

a. Opportunities have an objective component and their existence does not depend on whether the individual identifies these opportunities or not.

b. Every individual is different from others. Therefore, different individual has different ability of recognizing opportunities. In addition, according to the discovery theory, individuals are always alert to the existing opportunities and this alertness is not a deliberate search, but the constant scanning of environment by individuals.

c. Risk bearing is an essential part of the entrepreneurial process. The first and second assumptions of the discovery theory also support the risk bearing condition of entrepreneurship. As per these two assumptions, individuals can only discover and avail opportunities, but cannot create opportunities. They apply a unique combination of resources, means they do things differently to bring innovation.

As there is no certainty about the success of discovered opportunity, entrepreneurs bear risks by availing opportunity on the estimated probability of its success. Thus, the discovery theory states that opportunities are objectives, individuals are unique, and entrepreneurs are risk bearers.

2. Creation Theory:

Creation theory focuses on entrepreneurs and the creation of enterprises. Similar to the individual/opportunity nexus, the creation theory also approaches three assumptions in entrepreneurship.

The three assumptions are as follows:

a. Opportunities are subjective in nature. The creation theory also emphasizes that opportunities are created through a series of decisions to exploit a potential opportunity. This theory asserts that opportunities do not have an existence without the actions of entrepreneurs. The creation theory is opposite to I/O nexus.

The I/O model asserts that opportunities are discovered by scanning the business environment and analyzing the market and industry structure. On the other hand, the creation theory supports the view that opportunities are created by hypothesis testing and learning.

For example, consumer electronics organizations, such as Samsung, creates opportunities by developing new products, trying out those products in the market, finding out the products that are reasonably successful, and filtering the successful products and improving their marketability.

b. Opportunities are not recognized by individuals, but created by them. The creation theory suggests that entrepreneurship does not require differences in individuals, but differences in their decision making under uncertainty. According to the creation theory, an entrepreneur is someone, who organizes resources after evaluating the value of probable outcomes.

c. Individuals bear uncertainty not risk. The creation theory suggests that entrepreneurs create opportunities and act on them after estimating the probability of their success. Thus, bear uncertainty not risk.

Thus, the creative theory suggests that opportunities are subjective, individuals are ordinary, and entrepreneurs are uncertainty-bearers.

3. Economic Theories of Entrepreneurship

The economic theory is among the main theories of entrepreneurship. This theory asserts that the economy and entrepreneurship are closely linked together. Entrepreneurship and economic growth can only work when the economic conditions are favourable. As such, it is usually hard for entrepreneurs to realize growth when the economy is doing poorly. This theory further states that entrepreneurs find motivation in the presence of economic incentives which include industrial policy, policies of taxation, financial and resource sources, availability of infrastructure, investment opportunities, marketing opportunities, availability of information regarding the conditions of the market and technology among others . An entrepreneur is therefore a risk taker because he can never fully predict about the favourability of the economic conditions in future.

The economic entrepreneurship theory has deep roots in the classical and neoclassical theories of economics, and the Austrian market process (AMP). These theories explore the economic factors that enhance entrepreneurial behaviour. They are:

(a) **Classical Theory**

The classical theory inscribed the merits of free trade, specialisation, and competition (Ricardo, 1817). The classical movement described the directing role of the entrepreneur in the context of production and distribution of goods in a competitive marketplace (Say, 1834). Classical theorists articulated three modes of production: land; capital; and labour. There have been objections to the classical theories as the theorists failed to explain the dynamic disturbances generated by entrepreneurs of the industrial age (Murphy, Liao & Welsch, 2006).

(b) **Neo-classical Theory**

The neo-classical model emerged from the criticisms of the classical model and indicated that economic phenomena could be relegated to instances of pure exchange, reflect an optimal ratio, and transpire in an economic system that was basically closed. The economic system consisted of exchange participants, exchange occurrences, and the impact of results of the exchange on other market actors. The importance of exchange coupled with diminishing marginal utility created enough momentum for entrepreneurship in the neoclassical movement. Some criticisms were raised against the neo-classical as follows: the first is that aggregate demand ignores the exceptionality of individual-level of entrepreneurial activity. Secondly, neither use nor exchange value reflects the future value of innovation outcomes. The third point is that rational resource allocation does not capture the complexity of market-based systems. The forth point raised was that, efficiency-based performance does not subsume innovation and non-uniform outputs; known means/ends and perfect or semi-perfect knowledge does not describe uncertainty. In addition, perfect competition does not allow innovation and entrepreneurial activity. The fifth point is that it is impossible to trace all inputs and outputs in a market system. Finally, entrepreneurial activity is destructive to the order of an economic system (Murphy, Liao and Welsch, 2006).

(c) **Austrian Market Process (AMP)**

Austrian Market process (AMP) came into existence as a result of the short comings pointed out in neo-classical model. The AMP, a model championed by Joseph Aloi Schumpeter (1934) concentrated on human action in the context of an economy of knowledge. Schumpeter described entrepreneurship as a driver of market-based systems. This means that the major role of an enterprise is to produce something new which will result in processes that will serve as impulses for the movement of market economy. Murphy, Liao, & Welsch (2006) challenged that the motion offered a logic self-motivated reality. They explained this by pointing to the fact that knowledge is communicated throughout a market system, innovation transpires, entrepreneurs satisfy market needs, and system-level change occurs. If an entrepreneur knows a better way of improving on existing goods and services or to create new ones, benefits can be reaped through this knowledge. Entrepreneurs accomplish something when they believe it will obtain some individually-defined benefits. The earlier neoclassical framework did not explain such activity rather; it assumed perfect competition, carried closed-system assumptions, traced observable fact and inferred repeatable observation-based principles. On the contrary, AMP denied assumptions that circumstances are repeatable, always leading to the same outcome in an economic system. AMP held that entrepreneurs are motivated to use periodic knowledge (that is, possibly never seen before and never to be seen again), to generate value. Thus, it was based on three main conceptualizations (Kirzner, 1973).The first was the arbitraging market in which opportunities emerge for given market actors as others overlook certain opportunities or undertake suboptimal activity. The second was alertness to profit-making opportunities, which entrepreneurs discover and entrepreneurial advantage. The third conceptualization, according to Say (1803) and Schumpeter (1934), was that ownership is distinct from entrepreneurship. In other words, entrepreneurship does not require ownership of resources, an idea that adds context to uncertainty and risk (Knight, 1921). These conceptualizations show that every opportunity is unique and therefore previous activity cannot be used to predict outcomes reliably. The AMP model is not without criticisms. The first of the criticisms is that market systems are not purely competitive but can involve antagonist cooperation. The second is that resource monopolies can hinder competition and entrepreneurship. The third is that fraud /deception and taxes/controls also contribute to market system activity. The fourth is that private and state firms are different but both can be entrepreneurial and fifth, entrepreneurship can occur in non-market social situations without competition. Empirical studies by Acs and Audretsch (1988) have rejected the Schumpeterian argument that economies of scale are required for innovation. The criticisms of the AMP have given impetus to recent explanations from psychology, sociology, anthropology, and Management.

4. Sociological Theories of Entrepreneurship

This is also among the contemporary theories of entrepreneurship. It argues that the success of an entrepreneur is affected by their social culture. In other words, entrepreneurship is likely to get a boost in a particular social culture. They are more likely to achieve growth in particular social settings. Among the social aspects that affect an entrepreneur include the social values, customs, taboos, religious beliefs and other cultural activities. An entrepreneur perform base on social expectations when carrying out business.

Four social contexts that relate to entrepreneurial opportunity are as follows:

(a)   Networks: here, the focus is on building social relationships and bonds that promote trust and not opportunism. The entrepreneur should not in any way take undue advantage of people to be successful; rather success comes as a result of keeping faith with the people.

(b)   The life course stage context which involves analyzing the life situations and characteristic of individuals who have decided to become entrepreneurs. The experiences of people could influence their thought and action so they want to do something meaningful with their lives.

(c)   Ethnic identification. One's sociological background is one of the decisive "push" factors to become an entrepreneur.

(d)   Population ecology. The idea is that environmental factors play an important role in the survival of businesses [enterprises] and entrepreneur (Reynolds (1991).

Some of the sociological theories are as follows:

a. Theory of Religious Belief:
Max Weber propounded the theory of religious belief. According to him, entrepreneurial activities are functions of religious beliefs and impact of religion shapes the entrepreneurial culture. He emphasized that entrepreneurial energies are exogenous supplied by means of religious beliefs. Some of the important elements of Weber's theory are described as:
i. Spirit of capitalism – Spirit of capitalism is highlighted in the Weber's theory. It is generally known that capitalism is an economic system in which

economic freedom and private enterprise are overvalued, so also the entrepreneurial culture.

ii. Adventurous spirit – Webber also made a distinction between spirit of capitalism and adventurous spirit. According to him, the former is influenced by the strict discipline whereas the latter is affected by free force of impulse. Entrepreneurship culture is influenced by both these factors.

iii. Protestant ethic – According to Max Webber the spirit of capitalism can be grown only when the mental attitude in the society is favourable to capitalism

iv. Inducement of profit – Webber introduced the new businessman into the picture of tranquil routine. The spirit of capitalism intertwined with the motive of profit resulting in creation of greater number of business enterprises.

b. Theory of Entrepreneurial Supply:

Thomas Cochran concluded that cultural values, role expectation and social sanctions are key elements that determine entrepreneurs supply.

c. Theory of Social Change

This theory is developed by Everett E. Hagen. It explains how a traditional society becomes one in which continuing technical progress takes place. It exhorts certain elements which presume the entrepreneur's creativity as the key element of social transformation and economic growth. It reveals a general model of the society which considers interrelationship among physical environment, social culture, personality etc.

According to Hagen, most of the economic theories of underdevelopment are inadequate. Hagen insisted that the follower's syndrome on the part of the entrepreneur is discouraged. This is because the technology is an integral part of socio cultural-complex, and super-imposition of the same into different socio-cultural set-up may not deliver the goods.

5. Entrepreneurship Innovation Theory

This theory was propounded by J.A. Schumpeter. In Schumpeterian theory, the main theme is the innovation. He pointed out dissimilarity between an innovator and an inventor. According to him, an inventor discovers new methods and new materials. But, an innovator is one who applies inventions and discoveries in order to make new combinations. With the help of these new combinations, he produces newer and better goods which yield satisfaction as well as profits. According to Schumpeter, entrepreneurs do not just do business to better their lives alone rather, through their activities; they are able to cause development in the economy and the society at large. In a nut shell, an entrepreneur grows by being creative and having a foresight. One of the creative things that an entrepreneur does is introduce a new product which often comes to solve a certain problem in the society or make it more convenient. Another innovative aspect is that in a bid to achieve growth and have more profits, an entrepreneur introduces a new production method. Notably, enhanced production methods lead to a reduction in the cost of production and an increase in the goods manufactured. Innovation also comes in when an entrepreneur opens a new market. This is often done after the identification of a growth opportunity or a void in the economy. The discovery of new sources of raw materials and establishment of organization are also aspects of entrepreneurs being innovators. These activities of an entrepreneur lead to the creation of jobs and accessibility of commodities, thus improving the economy. Schumpeter's concept of entrepreneurship includes not only the independent business men but also executives and managers who actually undertake innovative functions.

Going by the above statements, it can be said that innovation occurs when the entrepreneur:

i. Introduces new products

ii. Introduces new methods of production

iii. Opens new market

iv. Conquests of new source of supply of raw material

v. Carrying out new organization

Limitations of Schumpeter's theory are as follows:

(i) It excludes individuals who merely operate an established business without performing innovative functions.

(ii) Innovating entrepreneur represents the most vigorous type of enterprise (R&D and innovative character). However, this type of entrepreneur character is rarely available in developing countries

(iii) It laid too much emphasis on innovative functions. But it ignores the risk taking and organising aspects of entrepreneurship.

(iv) It assumes an entrepreneur as a large scale business man. He is a person who creates something new. But in practice, not all the entrepreneurs have large scale operations from the very beginning, especially, in developing countries, where most entrepreneurs are small scale businessmen who need to imitate rather than innovate.

(v) The theory has the scope of entrepreneurism in the sense that it has included the individual businessman along with the directors and managers of the company.

(vi) It fails to provide a suitable answer to question like— why some countries had more entrepreneurial talent than others?

According to Schumpeter, entrepreneurs are not a class in themselves like capitalists and workers. An individual is an entrepreneur only when he actually carries out new combinations and ceases to be an entrepreneur the moment he settles down to running the established business.

According to Schumpeter, an entrepreneur exists only if the factors of production are combined for the first time. Maintenance of a combination is not an entrepreneurial activity. In this way, combination theory differs from the theory of rent formulated by Ricardo. Ricardo included the term "entrepreneurial ability" as an independent factor of production and it is concerned with profit. Thus, this theory fails to provide suitable solutions to the problems.

6. Psychological Theory of Entrepreneurship

The individual is the level of analysis in psychological theory. According to this theory, an entrepreneur experiences growth when the society has several individuals with the necessary psychological characteristics. These characteristics include having a vision, being able to face opposition and having the need to achieve highly. A person can only possess these traits during their upbringing, when they excel, when they are self-reliant and when there is low father dominance. They argued that both the factors of the environment and some inner motives within the individual are the main motivations for business pursuits. Empirical evidence presented three other new characteristics that have been found to be associated with entrepreneurial inclination. These are risk taking, innovativeness, and tolerance for ambiguity (Landstrom, 1998).

(a) *Need for Achievement theory*

Psychological theories of entrepreneurship focus on the individual and the mental or emotional elements that drive entrepreneurial individuals. A theory put forward by psychologist David McCLelland, (1961) a Harvard emeritus professor, offers that entrepreneurs possess a need for achievement that drives their activity. In other words, Need for achievement theory explained that human being have a need to succeed, accomplish, excel or achieve. He identified two characteristics of entrepreneurship which are: doing things in a new and better way and taking decisions under uncertainty. Entrepreneur *is driven* by this need to achieve and excel. He stresses that people with high achievement orientation have to succeed because they are not influence by money or external incentives. They consider profit as a measure of achievement and proficiency.

(b) Personality Traits theory

Personality traits are stable qualities that a person shows in most situations. Trait theorists believe that there are enduring inborn qualities or potentials of the individual that naturally make him an entrepreneur. The trait model is still not supported by research evidence. The only way to explain or claim that it exists is to look through the lenses of one's characteristics/behaviours and conclude that one has the inborn quality to become an entrepreneur. Some of the characteristics or behaviours associated with entrepreneurs are that they tend to be more opportunity driven (they nose around), demonstrate high level of creativity and innovation, and show high level of management skills and business know-how. They have also been found to be positive, Emotionally resilient and have mental energy, they are hard workers, show intense commitment and perseverance, thrive on competitive desire to excel and win, tend to be dissatisfied with the status quo and desire improvement, entrepreneurs are also transformational in nature, they are lifelong learners and use failure as a tool and springboard. They also believe that they can personally make a difference, are individuals of integrity and above all visionary. The trait model is still not supported by research evidence. The only way to explain or claim that it exists is by becoming an entrepreneur.

tone looks through the lenses of one's characteristics/behaviors and conclude that

(c) Locus of Control

Locus of control is an important aspect of personality. The concept was first introduced by Julian Rotter in the 1950s. Rotter (1966) refers to Locus of Control as an individual's perception about the major causes of events in his/her life. In other words, a locus of control orientation is a belief about whether the outcomes of our actions are dependent on what we do (internal control orientation) or on events outside our personal control (external control orientation).

Individuals with an internal locus of control believe that they are able to control life events, while individuals with an external locus of control believe that life's events are the result of external factors, such as opportunity, destiny or fate.

Empirical findings that internal locus of control is an entrepreneurial characteristic have been reported in the literature (Ho and Koh, 1992; Koh, 1996; Robinson et al., 1991). In a student sample, internal locus of control was found to be positively associated with the desire to become an entrepreneur (Bonnett & Furnham, 1991). Rauch and Frese (2000) also found that business owners have a slightly higher internal locus of control than other populations. Other studies have found a high degree of innovativeness, competitive aggressiveness, and autonomy reports (Utsch et al., 1999).The same is reported of protestant work ethic beliefs (Bonnet and Furnham, 1991).

7. Theory of high achievement/Theory of achievement motivation

Not all people are interested in being entrepreneurs. But David McClelland argued that people who aim to become entrepreneurs must have a need for achievement, a need for affiliation and a need for power. These act as the basis upon which an entrepreneurial personality is established. Achievement motivation has a lot of significance in entrepreneurship because it leads to economic and social development. Entrepreneurs always want to achieve success in their endeavors. The need for power comes from the urge to gain dominance in a certain field and thus cause influence among other people. The need for affiliation comes from the urge to motive or maintain friendships with other people. Notably, the need for achievement stands out amongst the others. It was identified through an experiment known as Kakinada Experiment by David McClelland. This experiment was conducted in Mexico, America and India. David McClelland gathered young adults who underwent training for 3 months. The goal was to induce achievement motivation. He asked them to have a positive thinking and assume as though they wanted success yet were facing various challenges. They were also asked to emulate their role model. At the end of the study, David McClelland came up with two conclusions about the characteristics of entrepreneurs. The first was that entrepreneurs do things in new and better ways. The second was that they make decisions under uncertain conditions. High achievement motivation is a sign that an individual is likely to become an entrepreneur because they are passionate about it. As such, even though they are stressed, lack money or face external pressures, they will work hard to become successful. Additionally, through the experiment, it was found out that the performance of an entrepreneur can be enhanced through education and training.

8. Resource Based Theories

According to these theories; entrepreneurs require resources to go about their businesses. Their efforts must be combined with resources such as time, money and labour. Failure to access resources can cause their efforts to become futile. Capital, for instance, enables an entrepreneur to grow their business. Other aspects that can be considered as essential resources include access to information, education and leadership. This theory stresses the importance of financial, social and human resources.

(a) **Financial Capital/Liquidity Theory** This theory argues that entrepreneurs have individual-specific resources that facilitate the recognition of new opportunities and the assembling of new resources for the emerging firm.

(b) Social Capital or Social Network Theory Entrepreneurs are embedded in a larger social network structure that constitutes a significant proportion of their opportunity structure. In a similar vein, Reynolds (1991) mentioned- social network in his four stages in the sociological theory. The literature on this theory shows that stronger social ties to resource providers facilitate the acquisition of resources and enhance the probability of opportunity exploitation

(a) Human Capital Entrepreneurship Theory Underlying the human capital entrepreneurship theory are two factors, education and experience (Becker, 1975). The knowledge gained from education and experience represents a resource that is heterogeneously distributed across individuals and in effect central to understanding differences in opportunity identification and exploitation.

9. Opportunity based theory

With the aim of being successful, entrepreneurs grab any opportunity they come across. These opportunities are made available through the changes in technology, society or culture. Notably, as these changes occur, consumers change their preferences. An entrepreneur must therefore take those changes as opportunities of succeeding in their businesses. Also, technology sets a basis upon which innovation is created and facilitated. Therefore, this theory suggests that entrepreneurs are always on the lookout for opportunities that will enable them increase the growth of their ventures

10. Status Withdrawal Theory

This theory argues that entrepreneurial aggressiveness can be created when people of a certain class lose the prestige they initially had or when they belong to a minority group. Entrepreneurship, if done correctly, can help a person live a satisfactory and content life. Therefore, individuals will attempt by all means to become as prestigious as they were in the past. If they come from a minority group, they must better their lives by working hard at being entrepreneurs. Also, being a successful entrepreneur evokes respect from the society. Producing an innovative product or service that will help solve various societal concerns can make a person to be highly valued and admired by the community. As such, some people aim at achieving this admiration, fame or popularity through entrepreneurship.

11. Anthropological Entrepreneurship Theory.

Anthropology is the study of the origin, development, customs, and beliefs of a community. In other words, the culture of the people in the community The anthropological theory states that for someone to successfully initiate a venture the social and cultural contexts should be examined or considered. Here emphasis is on the cultural entrepreneurship model. The model says that new venture is created by the influence of one's culture. Individual ethnicity affects attitude and behaviour (Baskerville, 2003). Also, cultural practices lead to entrepreneurial attitudes such as innovation that also lead to venture creation behaviour. Thus, cultural environments can produce attitude differences as well as entrepreneurial behaviour differences.

12. Financial Capital/Liquidity Theory

Study has shown that springing up of new firms is more common when people have access to financial capital (Blanchflower et al, 2001). This theory suggests that people with financial capital are more able to obtain resources to effectively take advantage of entrepreneurial opportunities, and set up a firm to do so (Clausen, 2006).

However , other studies contest this theory as it is demonstrated that most founders start new ventures without much capital, and that financial capital is not significantly related to the probability of being nascent entrepreneurs (Hurst & Lusardi, 2004,).This apparent confusion is due to the fact that the line of research connected to the theory of [illegible] to resolve whether a founder's access amount of capital employed to start a new venture Clausen (2006). In his view, this does not necessarily rule out the possibility of starting a firm without much capital. Therefore, founders access to capital is an important predictor of new venture growth but not necessarily important for the founding of a new venture (Hurst & Lusardi, 2004) This theory argues that entrepreneurs have individual-specific resources that facilitate the recognition of new opportunities and the assembling of new resources for the emerging firm (Alvarez & Busenitz, 2001). Research shows that some persons are more able to recognize and exploit opportunities than others because they have better access to information and knowledge (Anderson &Miller, 2003).

Conclusion

The purpose of this chapter was to examine the theories and research outcomes of entrepreneurship. From the above discussions it is clear that the field of entrepreneurship have some interesting and relevant theories (ranging from economic, psychological, sociological, anthropological, opportunity-based, to resource-
based) which are underpinned by empirical research evidence. This development holds a rather brighter future for the study, research, and practice of entrepreneurship.

It is critical for aspiring library entrepreneurs to know these theories. This can help them in knowing what to expect and the field in which they should exercise their entrepreneurial skills and abilities.

CHAPTER THREE
PUBLISHING

To publish means to make information and literature available for the public to view. Publishing involves the process of producing and distributing literature so that the public can have access to it. Sometimes, certain authors publish their own work and in that case they become their own publishers.

Publishing is a generic term that signifies the wide process of development/acquisition, production and dissemination of information. It is the activity of making information, literature, music, software and other content available to the public for sale or for free. Traditionally, the term refers to the distribution of printed works, such as books, newspapers, and magazines. Wikipedia

The traditional meaning of the word "publishing" means to print newspapers and books on paper and distribute them. the occupation or activity of preparing and issuing books, journals, and other material for sale. But now with improved technology we have the Internet and other digital information systems. So, now publishing is done not only through printing but also electronically. Of late a large number of periodicals and books have been published online and electronically through CDs and DVDs.

The authors of traditional printed materials sell exclusive territorial intellectual property rights that match the list of countries in which distribution is proposed (i.e. the rights match the legal systems under which copyright protections can be enforced). In the case of books, the publisher and writer must also agree on the intended formats of publication mass-market paperback, "trade" paperback and hardback are the most common options.

Who are publishers?

Publishers manage the manuscript editing, design and production process, using a team of editors, proofreaders, graphic designers and printers. They provide schedules for each stage of the process, working backwards from the planned publication date. The publisher is the one who usually controls marketing tasks such as advertising. If it is a small company, tasks such as proofreading, editing and layout may be outsourced to freelancers.

A publisher will need to select marketable material from a pile of submitted works, most of which are likely to be rejected before even being considered for publication if they are not of the genre their company specialises in.

One of the biggest choices an author is to make in career is choosing which publishing option to pursue. This will permanently shape the future of the author's writing. Understanding all the options before making final decision truly is a key to successful publishing.

Book publishers take responsibility for all aspects of book publication. Their aim is to attract good authors and publish books that achieve commercial success. Depending on the size of the publishing company, the book publisher may carry out all aspects of publication, or may delegate part of the work to editors, designers and marketing specialists.

Publishing offers career opportunities to people with a range of skills. Depending on their experience and qualifications, publishing staff may take responsibility for commissioning manuscripts for books, magazines or online content, editing, designing and preparing manuscripts for publication, or marketing the finished works. Publishing offers both full-time and freelance opportunities for roles such as copy editing, proofreading and design.

Steps Involved in Publishing

There are several steps involved in publishing process. For instance, if you want to publish a book, there are several steps involved in the process. The steps involved in publishing are development, acquisition, editing, designing of cover etc, production (which involves printing on paper or electronically), marketing and distribution.

Submission of Proposal
The author or the literary agent has to submit a proposal or query letter

Negotiation

Once the proposal has been accepted, the commissioning editors start to negotiate the purchasing of intellectual property rights and finally agree on a certain rate.

Editorial Stage

In this stage of publishing, the work to be published is reviewed and proofread and if any changes are to be made the author is asked to rewrite or make few changes. This is done usually to match the grammatical requirements and style of each market. Requesting for additional information and structural changes are part of this stage of publishing.

Prepress Stage

Once the text is finalized, the design has to be decided. Artwork, photographs and layout need to be finalized. Typesetting is done for placement of artwork and setting the layout. Proofreading is done in this stage of publishing also. Paper quality, composition of dust jacket and binding method has to be decided. Once typesetting is done, the files are saved normally in the PDF or whatever format that is also very reliable/suitable

This is a simple overview of what it takes to publish a book. If you successfully publish one book, you can start thinking about a reprint or about publishing a new book!

Forms of Publishing

There are various forms of publishing which must be put into consideration especially by the beginners before diving into the industry. They are:

Traditional Publishing

A traditional book publishing company buys the rights to an author's manuscript. Buying rights from the author is how book publishers have traditionally acquired books. Usually an agent, representing the author, negotiates the deal with the book publisher and in return gets a percentage of any income earned from the sales of the book. Part of the arrangement includes advance payment by the book publisher to the author to secure the book deal. In return, the author, working with an in-house editor, is expected to finish writing the book in an allotted time – which is often years away. The advance is deducted by the book publisher from any royalties the author receives from the sales of the book. Royalties are based on an agreed percentage of sales. The author does not receive any royalties until the advance is paid back in full. The book publisher budgets funds to promote and market the book – this amount varies greatly depending on the marketability of the book. The author is often strongly encouraged to hire a book publicist and to work aggressively to promote their book. The book publisher has the final say on every aspect of the author's book, from editorial content to cover design to the number of books in the first printing. The book publisher makes the determination, based on declining sales, as to when to allow a book to go out of print – this could be as short as a year or even less. Authors beware – some traditional publishing houses are putting their out of stock or back-list titles into commercial print on demand systems so the book isn't technically out of print and the book's rights will never revert back to the author.

Each day, agents and book publishers receive a staggering number of inquiries and manuscripts. Ultimately, less than 1% of authors seeking to be published traditionally are successful. Thousands of authors and their books are rejected daily. Of course, there are those authors who prefer not to get involved with the traditional book publishing world. Many of them enjoy the creative control and hassle-free experience of self-publishing (Infinity Publishing, 2020).

In traditional publishing (leaving aside digital variations on the theme), to publish a book, once the manuscript in question has been edited so that it is ready for print, is a matter of printing the book (creating pages with text or images or both on them) and then having the correctly arranged pages bound in one form or another (mostly either by gluing the spine or by sewing the pages together) and then offering the resultant product to the public for sale. This is what is called publishing.

Self Publishing

Self-publishing is not a new phenomenon. While most novels were distributed by established publishers, there have been authors who chose to self-publish, or even start their own presses. Just as the name implies, Self-publishing is the publication of media by its author without the involvement of an established publisher. The term usually refers to written media, such as books and magazines, either as an e-book or as a physical copy using POD (print on_demand) technology. It may also apply to albums, pamphlets, brochures, video content, etc.

Self-publishing unlike traditional publishing model, in which the publisher bears all the costs and risks of publication, but retains most of the profit if the book is successful. In self-publishing, the reverse is the case in that the author bears all the costs and risks, but earns a higher share of the profit per sale.

With new avenues of self-publishing, there are more opportunities for authors to break through directly to audiences for example, the rise of e-books and the arrival of Kindle from Amazon, has given authors direct access to millions of readers.

Before now, publishing has to go through agents and publishers but today, self publishing permits authors to bypass publishers and bookstores and sell directly to the public.

According to Henn (2015), The Internet has been described as a "great equalizer" in the publishing world, since it enables authors to put their books out there and "stand naked before the world especially now that costs for printing and distributing a book have fallen drastically. The emergence of new technologies in the past two decades has provided alternatives to traditional publishing. Self-publishing is increasingly becoming the first choice for writers. The quality of self-published works varies considerably, because there are no barriers to publication and no quality control.

Hybrid publishers

Under this form of publishing, an arrangement is made between traditional and self-publish in which both author and publisher bear some costs of development. This is sometimes called "cooperative publishing. In some cases, a hybrid publisher may offer selected services to help an author get a book published, such as proofreading, story editing, copy editing, , and marketing and public relations such as promotion through social media and search engine optimization strategies. Many such firms have their own online bookstores.

It is important for authors considering a hybrid approach to fully understand what services will be included, and at what cost, and to fully understand the terms of any contract before diving into it. Some intermediary firms offer less-than-ideal contracts, which make it hard for an author to get out of the deal at a later time, and can take a disproportionate share of profits. Authors therefore have to be careful when hiring such firms.

With this model, the author funds the publication of the book, sometimes spending a whole lot of money, to get the know-how and editing skills of the publisher. Quality of services and the terms of contracts vary widely. Some professionals who used to work in the traditional publishing industry work in hybrid firms. As a general rule, royalties are less than true self-publishing but more than traditional publishing. Books rarely get into bookstores. Authors should try to keep as many rights with as much flexibility as possible. Some firms are nothing more than assisted-publishing services which are overcharging.

Assisted self-publishing

These firms charge fees for various publishing-related services such as formatting and cover design and copyediting, and make their money from these services alone, but authors earn all of the royalties and retain control over editing and cover design and title. Firms that offer help with publicity and marketing are generally not a very good deal and firms that have pushy sales tactics such as Author-Solutions should be avoided. Would-be authors should look out for books on Self-Publishing for appropriate guide. For authors who are serious about making money through self-publishing, it is vital to have quality artwork, particularly on the cover, as well as interior formatting, and professionals doing publicity work, so hiring competent freelancers is critical.

True self-publishing

The author controls the entire publishing process from start to finish, and can hire freelancers to help with wherever the author requires, such as cover designers, copy editors, and story editors. It is necessary for the author to think like an entrepreneur and take charge of all variables, and as much as possible, get the finished book to look like a quality product. All profits and rights stay with the author but it is nearly impossible to get the book into bookstores unless it becomes a breakout bestseller, which is highly unlikely. Authors can sell their e-books through online platforms, and can distribute them through e-book distributors or print-on-demand firms.

Knowing the pros and cons of all the publishing routes is the key to making the best choice of writing career.

Process of self-publishing: from concept to manuscript (steps to publication)

Idea and concept

Writing

Rewriting

Story editing

More rewriting

Copyediting

Layout and typesetting

Cover design

Purchase an ISBN

Select platform(s)

Chose price

Choose distribution channel(s)

Upload

Marketing and promotion

Advantages of self-publishing

Speed: it is possible to avoid the process of finding a literary agent that will secure a publishing contract. An author can publish a book within two to three weeks avoiding unnecessary delay from publishers

Creative freedom: an author does not waste time trying to get published. There is no dull moment for a self-publisher once he finishes a book, he moves on to the next one.

Pitch books straight to the readers: there is no mediator suppressing ideas to be shown to the public. No restrictions in reaching readers

A greater share of royalties: royalty from the book sales is not meant to be shared with any publisher

Freedom to begin the next book: like earlier mentioned, there is no dull moment with a self-publisher, once he is done with a book, he goes on with the next one.

No start-up costs: Manuscripts uploaded to some platforms do not attract fees.

The Advantages of Traditional Publishing

Self-publishing is just as valid an option because there are indeed several advantages to traditional publishing that makes it more enticing option for many writers. They are as follows:

1. Literary Agents.

As a traditionally published author, your literary agent does more than just shop your manuscript around to publishing houses in hopes of snagging you a book deal. Your agent is your champion. They fight on behalf of you and your manuscript to help you get the most out of your traditional publishing experience.

Agents negotiate book deals and subsidiary contracts, cash advances, royalty rates, and other business-related matters. They also help manage an author's income affairs after their book deals have been signed, make sure authors stay on top of deadlines, and provide them with advice and encouragement as they navigate the industry.

Perhaps most importantly of all, agents mentor authors as they build their writing careers, helping them achieve long-term success in publishing.

2. A Team of Dedicated Professionals.

When an author inks a book deal with a publishing house, their book is assigned a team of professional editors, proofreaders, formatters, cover designers, marketers, and more that will help bring their book to life.

While self-published authors can (and should) hire professionals to help them as well, authors who choose traditional publishing don't have to pay a single dime upfront to work with their team.

3. No Upfront Costs.

In fact, traditionally published authors do not have to pay any upfront costs to publish their books. Should any agent or industry professional insist you pay them any sum of money, run the other way for they are certainly trying to scam you.

4. Cash Advances.

When an author signs a book deal, they'll likely receive a signing bonus called an advance. So long as the author fulfils their contract requirements, they are guaranteed to earn this advance regardless of how well their book sells after it has been published.

Advances for debut authors tend to fall between $2,000 and $15,000 USD, depending on many factors, the biggest been in the size and prestige of the publishing house. Advances are typically paid out in several instalments over the course of a year, most often after the author reaches major milestones in their publishing duties.

5. Greater Visibility and Reach.

While it isn't impossible for self-published authors to have their novels shelved in major bookstores, to negotiate international book deals and subsidiary rights, or to book author events like tours and readings, these opportunities are all far easier to attain when an author chooses to publish traditionally.

The visibility and reach traditional publishing provides can also help writers grow their careers faster than self-published authors, giving them a far greater chance of becoming a well-known name in fiction.

6. More Time to Write.

Self-published authors must coordinate everything involved in the publishing of their books, which can lead to less time spent on the actual act of writing.

However, traditionally published authors don't have to worry about organizing their book's cover design, blurb, formatting, copy-edits, etc. because their publishing house has already assigned their book to a team of experts.

7. Greater Opportunities for Acclaim.

In addition to having a better chance of becoming a well-known author, writers who choose the traditional publishing path also have more opportunities to win book awards, earn starred reviews, and land on bestseller lists.

8. Marketing Assistance

While most traditionally published authors must still market their books, they do have the opportunity to organize marketing plans with the team of experts at their publisher.

Additionally, as traditionally published authors' careers take off, it's far more likely that they'll receive additional marketing help as the publisher looks to capitalize as much as possible off of their success

9. Less Stigma

Unfortunately, there are still many readers who refuse to read self-published books because of the stigma surrounding them, which leads many to believe that self-published books aren't as high quality as those from big-name publishers.

There are also many readers who simply do not take the time to seek out self-published books. Publishing traditionally can help an author avoid this stigma and get their books in front of as many readers as possible.

The Disadvantages of Traditional Publishing

As it can be observed, there are quite a few advantages that come with pursuing a career in traditional publishing. But with those pros also comes a fair   share   of   cons.

1. LOWER ROYALTY RATES.

Unlike self-published authors, traditionally published authors don't get to keep all of the royalties from their book sales. In fact, an author will not even begin earning royalties until they make back their advance.

Traditionally published authors also don't receive 100% percent of their book's royalties. Both an author's publishing house and agent will take their own cuts of the profit. Typically, an agent takes 15% of all royalties, while the publishing house's cut will vary depending on the format, leaving the author to make about 10% on physical copies of their book and 30% - 40% on ebooks.

2. INFREQUENT PAY DAYS.

Publishing houses typically only pay out royalties twice a year, regardless of how well a writers' book sells. These infrequent pay days can, in some cases, complicate an author's financial life.

3. LOSS OF CREATIVE CONTROL.

Publishing houses almost always have final say in a book's cover design, title, back cover blurb, marketing angle, and more. Additionally, major disagreements concerning the direction of a story can arise between editor and author, making for a fraught publishing experience.

4. LONG PUBLISHING PROCESS.

When an author signs a book deal, their book is typically placed at the end of the publisher's publishing line-up, meaning it can take anywhere from 1 to 2.5 years for an author's book to finally arrive on shelves.

5. HARD BARRIER TO ENTRY.

Breaking into the publishing industry is extremely difficult. Writers can face dozens, even hundreds of rejections from both agents and publishing houses before their books are printed. Additionally, if their first book doesn't sell well, it can be even harder for an author to land subsequent book deals.

6. LOSS OF RIGHTS.

Unlike self-publishing, when an author signs a traditional book deal, they give away their rights to their book (in some cases, only for a certain period of time). This can cause many complications for an author for a number of reasons, particularly should an author disagree heavily with their publisher or should the publisher not want to pick up additional books in their line-up.

7. COMPLICATED CONTRACTS.

Any time an author signs with an agent or inks a deal for their book or subsidiary rights, complicated contracts come into play. In most cases, an author's agent will fight on their behalf to negotiate the best contract for everyone involved, but the tricky nature of legal contracts can always cause complications, especially if the author doesn't understand their rights before going into the signing process.

8. THE SHIFTING INDUSTRY.

The publishing industry is always changing. Market trends shift. Editors come and go. Members of an author's professional team switch houses, quit, get fired, or earn promotions. Publishing houses fold or merge. In some cases, the messiness that comes with the publishing industry can leave authors in a swing, throwing a major pull in their plans for their publishing career.

As you can see, traditional publishing truly is a give and take. Along with every fantastic advantage a traditional book deal provides, concessions must be made. But, of course, the same goes for self-publishing,

Self-publishing has many wonderful benefits that many writers should take into consideration before beginning to pursue publishing.

According to Jelusic (2003), There are several areas of possible cooperation between librarianship and publishing. The number of small and medium size publishers is growing, as are the number and diversity of titles published.

Commissioning Editor

Commissioning editors work closely with authors and other contributors, such as photographers or illustrators, to acquire manuscripts or visual content. They may work with regular contributors in addition to assessing proposals from new ones. When they are commissioning a project, editors provide contributors with contracts that set out editorial requirements, schedules and payment terms. They review each contribution in broad terms to ensure it meets the requirements of the contract.

Copy Editor

Copy editors review contributions for factual accuracy and check spelling, grammar and punctuation, liaising with contributors to resolve any queries. Then they prepare manuscripts for typesetting or digital production and check the final typeset manuscripts for accuracy. In larger publishing organizations, copy editors may work as part of a team using in-house or freelance proofreaders to carry out final manuscript checks.

Designers

Graphic designers work as part of an editorial and production team. They prepare layouts for magazines or books using contributors' text and visual material from photographers, illustrators or image libraries. Designers provide printers or digital production companies with detailed production specifications and check proofs for quality. They also design book or magazine covers and prepare promotional material, such as leaflets or website pages in conjunction with the marketing team.

Marketing

Marketing professionals create advertising and direct marketing campaigns to promote books and magazines to retailers, schools and colleges. They work closely with authors to promote their work through events, such as book signings and media interviews. Magazines offer career opportunities to media sales professionals, selling space to advertisers.

Profile

Some publishers concentrate on broad categories, such as fiction or non-fiction. Others specialize within those broad sectors, publishing non-fiction books on art, business or science, for example. The choice of subject may be based on tradition if the publishing company has a long history. Newer publishing houses base their lists on market conditions, modifying their publishing programs in line with market demand. Large publishing companies with a wide range of titles appoint a number of publishers, each with responsibility for a different category.

Authors

Book publishers may commission books that fit the profile of the publishing company. Or, they may review book proposals from authors or their agents. In larger companies, publishers delegate the detailed review of book proposals to commissioning editors, using their reports to make final decisions on whether to publish. Publishers prepare contracts that set out the requirements for the book and the payments the author will receive.

Editing and Design

When authors have completed their manuscripts, publishers review the text to ensure that it meets the requirements set out in the contract in terms of content, quality and length. Publishers manage the manuscript editing, design and production process, using a team of editors, proofreaders, graphic designers and printers. They provide schedules for each stage of the process, working backwards from the planned publication date.

Commercial Arrangements

Publishers may look for opportunities to sell copies of the book to book stores, schools and colleges, libraries, special-interest groups and book clubs. They also aim to sell overseas rights to other companies that will translate the text and publish the book in their own territories. They negotiate terms that give the publisher and author shares of the income from various groups. Typically, publishers offer authors a pre-publication advance on royalties from book sales and authors earn further royalties once sales revenue covers the advance. Sales revenue is based on the actual revenue the publisher receives, not the cover price of the book, because publishers give booksellers discounts of up to 50 percent. The income the publisher receives covers costs, including authors' royalties, production, distribution and overhead costs.

Promotion

To build sales of the book, publishers plan and manage a promotional program. They work with marketing and design professionals to create advertisements, direct marketing campaigns and other communications material. They publish book excerpts online, arrange interviews with authors and encourage authors to write opinion pieces for publication or participate in promotional events, such as book fairs, seminars and book store signings.

Publishing offers career opportunities to people with a range of skills. Depending on their experience and qualifications, publishing staff may take responsibility for commissioning manuscripts for books, magazines or online content, editing, designing and preparing manuscripts for publication, or marketing the finished works. Publishing offers both full-time and freelance opportunities for roles such as copy editing, proofreading and design.

According Orna, (2019), anyone who sets out to publish a book needs to understand the seven processes of publishing. Knowing the seven processes of publishing is useful because it allows you to see which ones you are good at and which you need to improve if you want to become a better publisher. Few people outside the business understand that being "published" is not a matter of somebody else deciding if your book is good enough. Book publishing is seven processes divided across three functions: making a book, selling books and licensing rights and formats.

The Seven Processes of Publishing: Three Functions

The three functions of publishing are making a book, selling it, and managing the rights that are bound up in that piece of intellectual property we call a book.

1. How do I master the editorial, design, and production tasks I can, need, and want to do?
2. What skills do I need to improve?
3. What skills *can* I improve, and which ones do I need to accept that I need help with?
4. Who do I get to help me? Where do I find good self-publishing services?
5. If I am self-publishing for the first time, will I use a full-service self-publishing company or assemble my own team of freelancers and publish directly to Amazon and/or others?
6. Where do I get feedback on my book, the cover, and other production matters?

Having mastered the intricacies of making a book, the author-publisher's attention then turns to reaching readers, book marketing, and promotion.

Selling the Book: Publishing Questions

This function includes distribution, marketing and promotion. Distribution is about who's going to take your book out to the world, make it available. Then marketing and promotion are about ensuring it is discovered.

Book marketing and promotion are often confused, or spoken of together, but they are not the same thing. Marketing centers on what the book publishing business calls "discoverability", ensuring that you and your books can be found by the right readers. It includes your author platform, your book covers and descriptions and reviews, your email list and digital funnels, and encompasses your promise to the reader. It's your marketing that allows readers to know what to expect from you and your books and it's an ongoing, ever-growing process.

Book promotion is time-based, a particular sales drive around a particular book. Promotions take many forms, including book launches, virtual or real-life book tours, advertising, and other purchased promotions. You are limited only by your imagination, time and money.

Questions

1. Which distributors and retailers am I going to use?
2. Who is my ideal reader?
3. What genres do I write in and who else writes in these genres?
4. What is my USP, the one thing I do that other authors don't do?
5. How do I best reach my ideal readers? What is my marketing plan?
6. How do I balance marketing and promotion tasks with writing more books?
7. How do I integrate the creative heart of my books into my marketing materials and sales pages?
8. Where do I best invest my resources of time and money?

Printing, publishing, and Copyright are they the same meaning?

The answer to the above question is capital 'NO'. Printing is a specific technology which could be part of the production sub-process of publishing.

Printing is simply the physical process of producing an image on paper or other medium. The printer gets paid for the work done and does not have to get the books in the shops. Publishing is more involved as it is, essentially, the link between the author(s) and the public.

Printing is usually for personal or short-term use. Publishing is a long-term business in which the publisher takes great pains to create a quality product that others will be willing to buy for years.

Copyright

Copyright gives the author a monopoly on copying and distribution of their work. This action is what we generally call "publishing". Copyright also prohibits others from publishing your work (without permission), so clearly they aren't the same thing.

Tips for beginners in publishing industry (conclusion)

Both traditional and self-publishing routes give authors the opportunity to share their stories with the world while building their writing careers. Publishing path to follow should not be decided on a whim.

We can all be better publishers. Like writing, publishing is an art and a craft that is never perfected. And technology has led to an explosion of tools and opportunities for authors which give room for endless improvement and expansion.

We all have our preferred reading format and many older readers, in particular, are passionate about print, loving the feel, the smell and the weight of a print book in the hand.

It is important to get our books into as many formats as possible so that the readers can choose their preferred format.

Decades back, books began as print and any electronic or audio version was handled as a "subsidiary" of that core format. Today's authors use digital tools to produce books in three formats: ebook (electronic), pbook (print), and abook (audio).

If it is your first book, it is advisable you move through the making and selling functions with an ebook, as that will set you up fastest for book sales. Ebooks are easiest and cheapest, and once you have mastered ebook production, you will have much of the materials and skills you need to produce print and audio, which are more expensive.

The production and sales processes across the three formats is similar, so once you have proven to yourself that you can make and sell ebooks, reinvest some of your profits into making the print book and audiobook editions, as soon as you afford to.

CHAPTER FOUR

PACKAGING AND REPACKAGING LIBRARY PRODUCTS AND SERVICES

Introduction

For librarians to survive in the face of modern technological and competitive world, they must rise up to trendy things by packaging and repackaging their products and services to the right user at the right time in the desired shape and required manner so as to attract high patronage.

Librarians have to bring to the market quality, profitable and informative products and services. The reason for all these is because librarians are encouraged to venture into entrepreneurship because that is the trendy thing. With the help of technologies, library services and products have to be presented in new dimensions. The target for this is towards making financial profit as it is obtainable in other organizations, to remain relevant in the face of competition as well as satisfying users' information needs. Therefore, the maintenance of optimum user patronage of library products and users' satisfaction derived from the product remains a watchword for every librarian. These products have to be repackaged in a way of rebranding.

Packaging is the process of designing and producing ....*product*. It is an important and effective sales tool for encouraging the consumers for buying a particular product. It is powerful medium for sales promotion. Also, packaging is the science, art and technology of enclosing or protecting products for distribution, storage, sale, and use. It also refers to the process of designing, evaluating, and producing packages.

Packaging trends are: Digital Printing Revolution, Personalized Packaging, Transparency and Clean Labels, Private Labels and Store Brands Dominating, Playful Colours, Designs and Gradients, Growth in Flexible Packaging, Recycled Packaging Products in Use, Vintage Packaging etc

Three P's of packaging are: protection, preservation, and promotion. Packaging exists to serve all these three elements. Library products are packaged so as to be protected preserved, promoted and make accessible by buyers (users)

Packaging of library products performs five basic functions and they are: Protection, Containment, Information, Utility and Promotion. All these put together gives a graduate librarian (intending entrepreneur) a better preparation before going into business world.

Information packaging has to do with providing the needed information resources to the intended clientele. By this, the knowledge managers retain their relevance and remain in business in the competitive world of information business.

The era of electronic information services and operations in libraries has called for information repackaging as a way of improving library services and meeting the needs and aspirations of users. For any library to repackage information and perform well and meet the needs of the users on this modern time, it is necessary for such a library to fully embrace the use of information and communication technology.
 Information repackaging therefore entails the selection and processing of information in a way that it will suite users using appropriate tools that communicate a message in a convenient and effective form for the user for whom it is intended.

Some scholars believe that information systems should actively get involved in the business of information repackaging other than only the traditional macro selection and accessing of information. There is need for the adoption of a system or pattern of making information seekers aware of the different formats of information resources available within the library, hence the need to satisfy the information needs of every user.

According to Obi and Anele (2020), Libraries have remained in the business of packaging information for quite sometimes but of recent, the advancements in technology and information explosion has given rise to information repackaging which is key in making the library and information centres an information reservoir for all and to make the library remain in business and relevant in the information industry. They went further in stating that the reasons for repackaging of library products and services through marketing are because library and information products and services are now being recognized as commodities that can be sold, exchanged, rent and transmitted. For the library to gain some level of self-sufficiency, it needs to think seriously about not only recovering the costs incurred but also making profits through their services to improve economy.

Information Packaging and Repackaging:

Over the years, there have been interpretations and counter interpretations with regards to information packaging of products and services which has become more complex and competitive, especially in recent times. The development of commercial society, industrialization, technological advancement, and the arrival of self-service meant that packaging had to be reinvented. It has become a medium of expression that follows strict codification system governed by rules and regulations, Packaging has become a medium of information between the library and the library users designed to speak and convince users to patronize the library.

Information repackaging is as old as the library itself it represents how an information service selects appropriate information resources, reprocess, and repackage the information and arrange such resources in a way that suits the user. Iwhiswho (2006) posits that information repackaging means, building of products and services to address specific needs of users.

The concept of information repackaging represents therefore organizing or processing of information in a form that can be understood by different categories of users. (Yahaya and Wesley, 2017). Information repackaging is a way of improving services and a systematic approach to the design and provision of information services appropriate to users' needs.

Importance of information repackaging in libraries

Information repackaging is a planned way of adding standards to library operations and services by way of creating awareness that is equivalent to the needs of library users. Information repackaging ensures currency, accuracy, appropriateness, comprehensiveness, ease of comprehension and convenience of use of information resources. Some key importance of information repackaging are:

- It facilitates dissemination, organization and communication of information resources
- It customizes information based on users need.

- It simplifies information.

- It facilitates interactivity between users, knowledge base and technology

Different forms of Information Repackaging

Different forms of information repackaging by Obi and Anele (2020) are explored as thus;

1. **Through user education/training on access to information product**: This is done in form of user education programmes or library orientation programmes. These programmes enable the users to be able to effectively explore the libraries and information centres to their own advantage.

2. **Audio Visual Resources**: Information could be repackaged through the use of audio visual resources to encourage learning, such as through photographs, filmstrips, paintings, video recordings, audio recordings, drawing, films, slides, motion pictures, bulletins, boards, etc.

3. **Through technological tools:** These include computer data bases, compact disks, CD Rom etc. Information technology represents the skill that permits dissemination of information at a greater value, effectively and efficiently to the world at large through a number of media platforms Adesanya (2002). Information is repackaged through the use of these tools.

4. **Reformatting and synthesizing raw information:** This means changing the original state of information as to make it easier for the user to understand.

5. **Through the use of songs:** different messages or information on varied issues can be used to compose songs in different languages. It must be in clear terms to depict the information to be transferred.

6. **Internet:** Information can be repackaged and circulated through the different internet connectivity. The internet is believed to offer a wide range of services which can enhance library operations and services. The e-commerce can be used to advertise different services and products available in the library through different medium.

7. **The Web:** Information on different subject areas ranging from library and information centres, services available, information on population, the world economy, sports and politics can be repackaged through this to all parts of the globe.

8. **The Social Media Platforms:** Such as Whatsapp, Facebook, Twitter, Instagrams, Youtube, and other platforms can enhance information repackaging in libraries.

Promotional tools for repackaged library Products and Services

Aderibigbe and Farouk (2017) posit that strategies to enhance effective marketing of library services include: publicity and public relation strategy, pasting of new information on the noticed board, enhancing the image of libraries, using user's orientation as a strategy, devising training programme, advertising in print media or directories, sending out newsletters, brochures and flyers, word of mouth, and also sales personnel by the libraries.

1. Personal skills: The Librarian needs to be professional, and adopt quality procedure, smile and establish personal relationship with users, react positively to complaints, think about users, suggestions instead of defending your position. Make yourself highly visible, visit staff rather than waiting for them to visit you. Learn research interest of staff, students and others; for these will go a long way.

2. E-mail: this is an easy way of reaching users quickly and cheaply. By maintaining up to date address lists by users, different user group can be targeted with different versions of the advertising message.

3. Internet: this internet has the power to improve the library's image and also allow the library to offer enhanced services. For example, a library web page serves as promotional tools for advertising in-house library services and electronic information resources and products on the web. Such page should include e-mail link to the library, making the librarians easy to contact.

4. Newsletters and Leaflets: these are also means of delivering information. A newsletter could be used to list interesting news web sites, new journals, and online services and general news of interest. These should be produced on regular basis and widely circulated to members of staff and students. Leaflets and guides can be handed out or displayed on notice boards. The library notice boards should be located in a prominent place.

5.   Telephone/SMS Platform are also good channels of promoting library products and services. Calling patrons and sending SMS message can go a long way in informing users about new books and services in the library.

Library Products

Information products are products that provide customers with information in a particular field. In library and information science, "information" can be seen as a consumable product that can only be consumed together with certain information delivery systems and/or services. The satisfaction of library users is a function of the quality of information product(s) received, the quality of information system and library services provided to access the information product. , information searching and retrieval activities are viewed as purchasing experiences of library users.

A product is an object, system and application which eases and enhances the quality of services provided by library and Information Centres to consumers. It is anything that can be offered to a market to satisfy the desire or need of customers. It can be ideas, goods, services, experience, organizations, persons, places, or a combination of two or more of these (Riyazuddi, 2012). Library products and services are the information carriers and strategies geared towards disseminating the contents of the products. Product can be in book or non book format and they include fiction books, non-fiction books, textbooks, newspaper/magazines, pictures and posters, records and tapes, audio and video, toys, CD-ROM and Braille materials etc.

Products are substantial, real, touchable or tangible. Products that are tangible can be shown easily, demonstrated, touched, displayed and are easier for users to understand and rate them in terms of value, usefulness and satisfaction while services are insubstantial, intangible, indefinable and vague. This means that services are not physical products that can be seen, touched and stored but can be experienced. Furthermore, when supplied products get to the consumer, it cannot come back to the producer unless in exceptional case whereby products are not delivered in good shapes meanwhile, services cannot be separated from the giver rather the quality may be improved upon from time to time.

Satisfaction got from a product by a consumer is a function of three main sources— quality of the information product, the information system and the services that make the information product available. These three measures of satisfaction are defined by the information resources, facilities and services. These sources of satisfaction, when properly harnessed may contribute to users' overall satisfaction. The accuracy, completeness, precision, and relevance of the information materials obtained by a user are measures of the product performance. According to De Aze (2002), products and services which provide benefits for users and which answer users' most important needs are the core business of the library and information service. Products of the library therefore are those equipment, facilities and resources made available to meet staff and users information needs. It could either be information or service based products.

Information products are therefore intellectual properties stored in any format suitable for selling and information products include: Webinars, Live events, Cheat sheets, online courses, E-books, Membership sites, Reports and analysis, Templates and teardowns, Live event recording and recaps while the services include community information services, recreational activities, reference services, storytelling, reading competition, career information, customer care, adult literacy education, mobile library services, and services to prisoners, online internet search, among others (IFLA, 2001).

Library products vary in format, size and shape. They are the information carrying documents (print and non-print) and equipments which are used to render library services. The products comprise books, journals, newspapers, magazines, DVDs, CDs, databases and databanks as well as reprographic machines. They also include Audio-Visual Materials (AVM) and Electronic Information Resources (EIR). Audiovisual (AV) products or multisensory materials which are library materials that permit the perception of information via the sensory organs of sight and hearing simultaneously (Akanwa, 2016). They consist of motion pictures, television programmes, video discs, computers, microforms, charts, models, radio, etc, while the digital or EIR are those library resources that are accessed electronically either on-line via the internet or through devices like the Compact Disc Read Only Memory (CD ROM), Digital Video Disc (DVD) or Compact Disc (CD). Reprographic/Electrostatic copying machines are available for making reduced or facsimiles of simple documents such as certificates, diagrams, scientific formulae, and journal articles cheaply and quickly. Other types of reprographic equipment include: Rank Xerox model, coronostat copier, savin copier, majox, microfilm camera, electro microfilm camera, Leica reprovit copying unit, microfilm processing unit, Photostat camera, Leica camera, auto fax, microfilm roll-to-roll, contact printer, contact document printer, microfiche camera, micro fiche reader, micro card camera.

Library Services

The intangibility of service makes it difficult to illustrate its values. According to Okorie (2020), service could be in form of business, personal or social services rendered in organisations. Library services are those strategies adopted to project the image of the library to the user community and to promote the goals and objectives of the parent institution. This image is the outcome of quality and effective services and also the ability to anticipate the desires and requirements of actual and potential users and their fulfilment. No wonder Narayana cited in Madhusudhan cited in Okorie (2020) points out that the, survival of a library depends among other things on its image in the minds of the users and the fund allocators.

Okorie (2016) categorized library services under two broad headings; conventional services and services for promoting library use. The author explains that while circulation services (charging and discharging functions) reprography and inter-library loan services are the conventional services, orientation services, reference services, current awareness/selective dissemination of information services, information brokerage, community information services, ICT related services, internet services, new arrival displays press clipping services are the services for promoting library use. Rowley (2006) also identified library services to include Information services, Document delivery and inter-library loan services, End-user training, Market research agencies, Information service providers (ISPs), Alerting services, Helpdesk services, Consultancy services, Financial and business information services, Entertainment services and Computing services. All these services are information-based services and as such can be privatized by graduate librarians that have the spirit of entrepreneurship in them. These services are tailored towards assisting individuals or group of persons to have equitable and easy access to information products.

Developments in Information and Communications Technologies (ICTs) and the Internet are two catalysts of change in the info environment. Their emergence to the society and their embrace by the library has transformed the traditional library services to more sophisticated information-based services. These services among others include: services providing access to databases, electronic current-awareness services, information brokerage, business consultancy services, subject gateways and portals, social services, reprography services, web-based information services, inter-library loan services, community information services, recreational activities, reference services, storytelling, reading competition, career information, customer care, adult literacy education, mobile library services, services to prisoners, online internet search and services to people with special needs. The above listed are some of the already existing packaged library services. In order to satisfy that human nature of always craving and yearning for new things, these services can be repackaged by library entrepreneurs for another income stream.

Circulation Service:

This is the heartbeat of every library it is usually found near the main entrance of a library. Activities carried out in this section; represent all the services related to accessing library materials these activities include: Check-out and check-in of materials, renewals, hold & recalls, book reserves, notifying and searching items, user assistance, registration of new members, issuing library clearance to departing users, shelving of materials, maintenance of collection in perfect order and shape, search, notify and recall.

No library is self sufficient for this reason, inter library loan is a welcome idea, it occurs when libraries enter into mutual agreement to provide users with information materials owned by another library. The user makes a request with their local library, which, acts as an intermediary, identifies owners of the desired item, places order, receives the item, makes it available to the user, and arranges for its return.

Library Liaisons Service

This service is peculiar to academic institutions but an individual can take it up as a personal business since its major aim is to bring the library and its services closer to the users and to promote academic programmes.

Reference Service

Reference services came into existence in response to the societal increasing demands to use volumes/varieties of information resources from innumerable library resources in different formats, to accurately and pleasantly meet people's information needs and satisfy their desire for knowledge and research. The major concern here is to provide instructions that will aid the patrons to become more independent in their use of the library. The following are some reference services provided by the reference librarian to the users of the library; guidance/advisory service, subject specialists' service, ready reference service, research consulting service, instruction service, outreach, bibliographic and citation service, documentation retrieval service and literacy programs. These services are rendered in response to patrons' reference questions or queries.

User Education Service

User education is a library orientation (instruction and training) given to new library users by the librarian to help them make maximum use of the library and its information sources. User education service can be formal or informal, instruction delivered by a librarian or other library staff members and this can be done one-on-one or in a group. The service covers both library training and information skills training and all the activities involved in teaching users on how to make the best possible use of library resources, services and facilities.

Information Service

Information services are rendered to assist customers with the use of the library's collections and databases. These services predict users' needs. These services include: various forms of bibliographic compilation, indexing, abstracting, current awareness services, selective dissemination of information, retrospective searching, and possibly, translating services. In fact, these are core library entrepreneurial services.

Selective Dissemination of Information (SDI)

SDI is a very dynamic personal current awareness and system selected information service that aims at providing research beneficiaries with the latest publications on research topics that reflect or fall within the scope of their interest on a regular basis. The service is an important part of library services that focuses mainly on library fundamental aim of providing the right information at the right time to right users.

Current Awareness Service (CAS)

Current awareness service is the act of informing clients of latest literature appearing in their specific fields of interest by providing regular updates on recently published materials whether they request for it or not.

Referral Services

Referral services have to do with helping to put patrons in contact with the best organization for their information needs. There is a saying that no one knows it or has it all. Clients often time have needs that neither you nor books alone can solve. In a situation such as this, referral services come to play.

Collection Development Services

Collection development is the process of carefully building up library products in the right quantity and quality among the overwhelming mass of information materials available throughout the world. It involves honesty in judging not only information materials but also readers to use the collections by considering their levels of education, reading interest and aspirations. Collection development includes assessing user needs, evaluating the present collection, determining selection policy, coordinating selection of items, weeding and storing parts of the collections and planning for resource sharing or cooperation. In the face of dwindling resources, collection development has to be done in such a way that information needs of the clienteles will be met.

Marketing Service

For a library to act as a window to the world of information and to promote quick access to its information content, marketing services are employed. Marketing is an integral part of library information-based products and service, because it has to do with basic principles of librarianship i.e. to provide accurate and up-to-date information, develop good collection and user-oriented services..

Information Communication Technology Services (ICTS)

Services that can be rendered through the use of ICTs are unsearchable. These are computerized services provided to reduce traditional ways of rendering services which were full of errors and time consuming. ICT-based library services include: CD-ROM Searching, Online Searching, Online Networking, Online Information Service, News Clipping Scanning Service, Database Searching Service, Photocopying service etc databases within the traditional library environment.

Press Clipping Services

Newspapers are the most important sources of latest information. Press clipping services involve cuttings of relevant write-ups, editorial letters, statements, news items, events etc. organized in some logical order for future reference and use.

Internet Services

Internet services are made available over the Internet for people to use and this has broken down the distance barrier in communication. This has greatly influenced the practice of librarianship. Internet is powerful and as such provides access to information from anywhere in the world at an unimaginable speed. Filtering software, printing, downloading, e-mail assistance, Wi-Fi services, bulletin boards, mailing lists, video conferencing, chat lines or rooms, games, Telnet, e-Commerce, etc. One of the main reasons for this type of service is to provide users access to another information resource. Provision of the opportunity to 'surf the net' or access the web is the baseline network service.

Remote Access Services

Remote Access Services (RAS) Server can be installed for networking with affiliated libraries and other institutions. Services such as OPAC, querying, ILL management, and electronic mail-based alert services can also be provided.

Digital Information Services

The severe shortage of periodicals faced by libraries for many years, due to the widening gap between the demand for literature and limited resources can be lessen through Digital Information Services by subscribing to content pages of different subject areas of many e-journals and databases from publishers/vendors such as: ACS Publications, JOSTOR, Emerald, etc.

Services to people with special needs

People with special needs include: people with visual or sight impairment, hearing impaired persons, Reading difficulty users, persons with physical disabilities, cognitively disabled persons, the deaf and dumb, the bind, the aged people etc. This class of people also have information needs like every other library user but it is quite unfortunate that most of the time they are neglected not being put into consideration whenever an arrangement is made probably because they belong to minority group.

In this case, a graduate librarian that has entrepreneurial spirit can look inward and find a way of rendering personal services to these categories of people by repackaging some library services for a fee. Specialized services could also be rendered based on the nature of disabilities. For example, by getting some library sign language videos for those who have hearing problems. For those that cannot walk, they can be served by sending books to them through mail, rendering reference services by fax or email, rendering home delivery service, Other services are volunteer readers and technology assistants. All these can be done for a fee.

Users with visual or sight impairment can be guided on how to find books and periodicals. They can be given the large type font and Braille guides, quick reference sheets on using the adaptive workstations, using the keypad to invoke the speech Information on audio tape, CD/DVD, or in DAISY format. While Audio information can be provided in text format and made available as text and easy-to-read text for patrons who are deaf.

Conclusion

Knowledge managers have been in the business of packaging information for years but of recent, the advancements in technology has called for information repackage which is key to making the librarians remain in business and relevant in the information industry. Product is the most important factor in library. Marketing library products and services is significant in a dynamic and competitive information environment. The library needs to modify, repackaged and market its products and services in order to remain relevant and promote her image.

The phrase library service entails how patrons are enabled to use the library and all it provides. The satisfaction of library users is a function of three main sources - the quality of information product(s) received; the quality of information system and library services provided to access the information product. Libraries offer a wide variety of useful information products, expertise and technologies.

CHAPTER FIVE

MARKETING A NEW VENTURE

Business Venture

Venture is both a noun and a verb. As a verb it means to go out, to do something or to undertake an activity involving risk while as a noun it means an initiative, a business, a project, a startup or a work that has some risks or uncertainty attached to it.

Many people refer to a business venture as a small business as it typically begins with a small amount of financial resources. Business venture is a new business that is formed with a plan or is a startup entity that has been created to generate a profit. Often, this kind of business is referred to as a small business and it is created when a need for a particular service or product is lacking in the market. This need is often a product consumers are requesting or something that serves a particular purpose. After the need is determined, an entrepreneur (librarian) with the time and resources to develop and market the new service or product can start a business venture. For example, a librarian can decide to open a business center close to a library so that library clients can easily go and get some services for a fee. Also, a librarian (entrepreneur) can decide to open a bookshop within or outside a school by so doing, students or lecturers can go there and get some books that they cannot find in their libraries. Most likely, the development will be funded in its early stages by an investor, who is often the business owner or creator of the idea (entrepreneur who is a librarian). Business ventures can sometimes be funded by more than one investor, with the expectation that the plan will be profitable in future.

Some of these small businesses that *LIS* professionals can *venture* into are: publishing, brokerage e-mail publishing, web publishing, and desktop publishing etc. *They can* resort to providing services that mainly deliver newsletters to consumers.

Marketing

Marketing is considered to be of utmost importance for the success of new ventures. The key to a successful marketing is by finding the right marketing strategy which includes: messages, timing, and method of communication that will reach and influence one's consumers on their decisions towards products or services.

Marketing is the study and management of exchange relationships. It is the business process of identifying, anticipating and satisfying customers' needs and wants. Because marketing is used to attract customers, it is one of the primary components of business management and commerce.

Marketing can therefore said to be the act of promoting and selling products or services, including market research and advertising. In a nutshell, marketing is the process of motivating would-be customers and clients of your products and/or services. The key word in this marketing definition is "process"; this is because, marketing involves researching, promoting, selling, and distribution of one's products or services. Marketing is all about profit making, little wonder why one of the maxims of marketing says that a profitable sales volume is more desirable than the maximum sales volume.

Marketing is all about attracting and retaining a growing base of satisfied customers. Creating and implementing a marketing plan will keep your marketing efforts focused and increase your sales
Lake (2019) in her opinion, sees Marketing as a process of teaching consumers why they should choose your products or services over those of your competitors; she sees marketing as a form of persuasive communication which is made up of every process involved in moving a product or service from your business to the consumer. Marketing includes creating the product or service concept, identifying who is likely to purchase it, promoting it, and moving it through the appropriate selling channels.

Basically, there are six primary purposes of marketing:

1. Identifying the customers' needs
2. Choosing the right product or service that can satisfy that need
3. Capturing the attention of your target market

4. Persuading a consumer to purchase your product

5. Providing the customer with a specific, low-risk action that is easy to take

6. Making a profit at the end of the whole activities or processes.

If the objective of your business is to sell more products or services, then marketing is what helps you achieve that goal. Anything that you use to communicate with your customers in a way that persuades them to buy your products or services is marketing. Marketing activities include advertising, social media, coupons, sales, and even how products are displayed.

As soon as one develops a marketing strategy, it is imperative for him/her to continually evaluate and reevaluate his/her business activities using the Seven P Formula which include: product, price, promotion, place, packaging, positioning and people.

The Ps Model of Marketing

The four stages of marketing can also be mapped onto another popular marketing model known as the Four Ps of marketing. The 4 Ps of marketing are considered to be the foundation of your marketing plan. They represent the main decisions you will have to make when marketing your products or services.

The four Ps in this model are product, price, promotion, and place. We will be looking at the traditional and digital marketing mix. Getting the marketing mix right means you will be able to align with your customers' wants and needs and also strengthen your brand presence.

The Traditional Marketing Mix

- **Product** – what will your product or service actually be and how does it meet the needs of your customer? The procedures you have in place to ensure that your products are ready for selling. Your product (or service) should fill a gap in the market, meet the needs of customers, and stand out from the competition.
- **Pricing** – The cost of purchase, including both the sticker price as well as less quantifiable trade-offs that a customer must be willing to make when they purchase your products has to be put into consideration. What price will you set your product at? This is not always a monetary figure as customers may exchange their time or information for a "free" product.
- **Place** – Refers to how and where products are sold. All distribution decisions are part of your overall marketing process. How do you deliver the product to the customer? Do they come into a physical store or do you sell online? Are you targeting a particular geographic region?
- **Promotion** – The information you give consumers through targeted advertising to generate interest in your products. Promotions usually have one of two purposes: generate leads or initiate actual purchases. What marketing methods will you use to tell the world about your product?

The Marketing Mix in the Digital Age

The concept of the 4Ps marketing mix was thought up well before the internet became a part of normal everyday life, but it can be adapted pretty easily to form the basis for developing a marketing strategy in today's digital world. In the digital marketing mix, the 4 Ps are the same, but the approaches are different.

- **Product** – The internet means that you can have a business with no physical inventory. Instead, you can sell digital products such as e-books and courses. Even if you do sell tangible products, the process of product development has been forever changed. It is now possible to order and create products on-demand to test out the market first, and the ability to survey your customers quickly and easily means you are less likely to make mistakes when it comes to product development.

- **Price** – Digital marketing technology means that you do not have to decide on a single price for your product or service – you can dynamically adjust the price depending on who is viewing it. There is also more flexibility when it comes to pricing models, with subscriptions and recurring payments made more accessible to businesses and customers of all kinds.
- **Place** – Clearly the main difference here is you are selling online instead of in a bricks-and-mortar store. But there are also many different channels to explore when it comes to selling online. Your own website, online market places, email, and social media are all avenues to consider.
- **Promotion** – Again, you will still promote your product but the methods are different from what you would have used years ago. Instead of direct mail and print advertising, your strategy might include email marketing and social media marketing instead.

In a nutshell, when a marketing program is being put together for one's business, it is advisable to concentrate on the basics, which are the key components of any marketing plan which are the: Products and Services, Promotion, Distribution, Pricing and places.

The rise of social media platforms have increased the importance of social media marketing, including connecting with customers on social media by persuading them to follow your business, partnering with social media influencers through product placement or paid sponsorships, and paying for advertising on platforms like Twitter or Instagram. The types of advertising to be choosing by an entrepreneur (librarian) will depend on his or her budget, type of business, and targeted customers.

The key to an organization's success, regardless of its size is marketing. Marketing process begins when an idea for a new product is conceived and continues until that product is in the hands of a consumer who bought it. Marketing is what you say, how you say it, how you package and present your product when you want to explain how amazing your product is and why people should buy it. Before a meaningful marketing takes place, a librarian (entrepreneur) must have understood his or her customers, then build and maintain relationships with them. This is because, even after a customer has made a purchase, marketing should not end a portion of advertising should be targeted at current customers to ensure they remain customers and increase loyalty. The entrepreneur has to make use of the type of marketing that will work best for him or her either online or offline.

The aim of marketing is to know and understand the customer so well the product or service fits him and sells itself. Marketing is about deep psychological understanding of customer needs. If business is composed of marketing and innovation, and marketing is about deep customer insights, then marketing is the job of every employee.

Social media has only made this point painfully clear: every employee is an extension of the brand. The brand serves to meet the needs of the customer and the business serves to innovate. Marketing starts by asking consumers who they are, what they want, and what they care about. Marketing starts with a question

Types of Marketing

Marketing these days can either be offline or online (digital methods). Offline marketing consists of "traditional" advertising in print, radio, and television marketing, as well as attending events like tradeshows, fairs and conferences. It can also include word-of-mouth marketing.

Most businesses will use a combination of online and offline marketing methods. However, these days the shifting is more towards online marketing. This is because consumers are increasingly spending more time online and digital marketing offers various advantages in terms of speed and efficiency.

Types of Online Marketing

- **Content marketing** – Publishing content in different forms to build brand awareness and nurture relationships with customers. Content marketing is usually thought of as a type of digital marketing but it can also take place offline. Examples of content marketing include blogs, posts on social media, info-graphics, and video.
- **Search engine optimization** – Commonly known as SEO, this is the process of optimizing the content on your website to make it more visible to search engines and attract more traffic from searches.
- **Search engine marketing** – Also known as pay-per-click or PPC, with this type of marketing businesses pay to have a link to their site placed in a prominent position on search engine result pages
- **Social media marketing** – Using social networks like Facebook, Instagram, and Twitter to build relationships with existing customers and reach a wider audience through digital word-of-mouth.
- **Email marketing** – Sending regular email communications to users who have signed up to your list to build relationships and drive sales.
- **Retargeting** – Contacting existing or potential customers after they have already had an interaction with your brand to get them to come back or convert into a sale. For example, placing an advert on their Facebook feed of a particular product they've looked at on your site.
- **Influencer marketing** – Using individuals with a high profile and many followers on social network channels to promote your product or service.

These are just a few examples of the most popular types of digital marketing in play today. Each of these methods can be broken down into several other types of marketing and there are indeed hundreds or thousands of different types of marketing covering both online and offline channels. No business relies on just one form of marketing. On the other hand, unless you're a multinational corporation with a practically unlimited budget and resources, it's not possible to tackle all different forms of marketing either.

To form an effective marketing strategy for your individual business, you must select the types of marketing that will be most effective for you, and form a plan in which they are integrated into a master strategy.

Understanding Your Customer

In marketing, knowing your customer is the key. In fact, some marketers go so far as saying that marketing is essentially the process of understanding your customers.

Marketing should start right at the beginning of your business journey, before your brand even takes form. This initial marketing involves research and learning more about your customers in order to develop a product or service that meets their wants and needs.

This in-depth customer research isn't a one-off marketing task, but one that is continuous. Focus groups, customer surveys, and collecting user data online are all ways that can help you to learn more about your evolving customer base and ensure that your brand is communicating with them in the right ways.

After a particular product or service has been introduced to the market, its success must be evaluated to see if it is meeting customer needs. Marketing also plays a part in customer service and nurturing customer relationships. It is not just about getting new customers, but also making sure you get the most out of your existing customers and that they stick around for as long as possible.

Digital marketing has opened up a new world of possibilities when it comes to understanding your customers better and building relationships with them. We now have the ability to collect a vast amount of data about individuals including their demographics, location, shopping habits, previous brand interactions, likes and dislikes, and lots more.

Four Stages of Marketing by Lake (2019)

Companies must go through multiple stages of marketing to ensure their products or services are ready for selling.

Ideation: Marketing starts when you develop an idea for a product or service. Before launching a product or services, you must decide what you are selling, how many options are available, and how it will be packaged and presented to consumers.

Research and testing: Before you can take your idea to the public, you should perform marketing research and testing. Marketing departments usually test new product concepts with focus groups and surveys to weigh consumer interest, refine product ideas, and determine what price to set. Researching your competitors can help you set an optimal price and generate ideas for positioning your brand in an existing market.

Advertising: Advertising is a marketing communication that employs an openly sponsored, non-personal message to promote or sell a product, service or idea or it could be a marketing approach involving paying for space to promote a product or service. The information you gather in your research will help you define your marketing strategy and create an advertising campaign. There are many types of advertising that one can use to promote business, teach customers about products, and generate sales. Print and non print campaigns are types of advertising. Campaigns can include different forms of media, events, direct advertising, paid partnerships, public relations, and more. Before beginning an advertising campaign, set concrete benchmarks that you can use to measure how effective that advertising campaign is. Some companies also use referral marketing, where satisfied customers refer others (sometimes for a reward) to increase business. The rise of social media platforms has increased the importance of social media marketing, including connecting with customers on social media by persuading them to follow your business, partnering with social media influencers through product placement or paid sponsorships, and paying for advertising on platforms like Twitter or Instagram. The types of advertising to be choosing by an entrepreneur will depend on his or her budget, type of business, and targeted customers.

Selling: Determine where and how you plan to sell to customers. Consumer product companies, for example, sell to wholesalers who then sell to retailers. In the industrial market, the buying process is longer and involves more decision-makers. You may sell locally, nationally, or even internationally, and some companies only sell their products or services online. Your distribution and sales channels impact who buys your products, when they buy them, and how they buy them.

Other stages include: Marketing Plans, Marketing Strategy and Distribution.

Marketing Plans: A Marketing Plan is the detailed activities to be taken in order to achieve the marketing objectives. Activities like: What, When, Who and How Much. After going through a marketing plan, one will be armed with information like: the things that will be done, when they will be done, who are the people to do them and how much the whole processes will cost.

Marketing planning process has to do with SWOT analysis, setting marketing goals, choosing a marketing strategy, giving details of what will be done in each of the 4Ps, implementing the plan and reviewing achievements.

Marketing Strategy: Basically, there are 4 Marketing Strategies and they are all about techniques to be employed in order to increase sales and profit.

(i) **Market Share Strategy**: Under this strategy, a business aims at increasing sales by selling more of its current products to current market. This situation arises when customers cannot get enough of the products or when the current products in the current market are preferred to that of competitors.

(ii) **New Market Strategy**: Here, a business tends to increase its sales by selling current product to a new market which could be a neighboring village, a park, school, hospital etc. This situation arises when customers in the new market cannot get enough of the products or when they prefer the products to that of competitors.

(iii) **Product Development Strategy**: Under this strategy, a business tends to increase sales by improving on existing product or by creating a new one. This could be as a result of the improved or new product being better than that of the competitors or still, this situation can spring up when nobody sells the new product in the current market or when customers cannot get enough it locally.

(iv) **Start-up/Diversification Strategy**: This type of strategy is a risky one because it involves both a new product and a new market. Under this strategy, the business is new and it wants to increase sales by selling a product to an entirely new market. For this type of business to succeed, the product must have a competitive advantage and there must also be a market opportunity for product diversification.

It is advisable for any business that wants to succeed to employ one strategy that gives it competitive advantage.

Distribution

Distribution means dispatching goods from the factory to the customers. It is all about making goods to get to the final consumer from the manufacturer through a distribution channel. Basically, the frequently used channels are:

- Producer – Wholesaler – Retailer – Consumer
- Producer – Retailer – Consumer
- Producer – Consumer

Some producers can decide to make use of more than one channel of distribution. The choice of channel to be used depends on: the type of product, who the customers are, where the customers stay, what the population of the customers is and how much they are to buy the product.

The type of product one produces determines the type of customers and places to sell the products. For example, if a product is a luxury one, majority of the customers will be well-to-do ones that mainly stay in the city but if the product is staple foods, the general public will be the customer meaning that the product can be sold everywhere through markets, stores, shops etc.

Middlemen

Middlemen are seen as sources of supply and points of contact with producers. They are intermediary between the producers and consumers to help in the distribution of products. Middlemen specialize in performing activities that are directly involved in the purchase and sales of products in the process of their flow from producers to the ultimate buyers. Their position is between the producers and ultimate buyers. They are important links between producers and consumers.

With the help of middlemen, products can be delivered easily, conveniently and efficiently to the consumers. The role of middlemen is to directly negotiate between buyers and sellers whether they buy the products or not. They are the furnishers of valuable information to the producers about consumer behavior, the changes in tastes and trends, etc. They make available the goods according to the consumers' needs, fashion, tastes, etc.

Examples of middlemen include: wholesalers, retailers, agents and brokers. Wholesalers and agents are closer to the producers.

Sales Representatives

Sales representatives also known as sales agents are critical to the manufacturers and wholesalers, as they are the ones that promote and market the merchandise for them. They give people idea about the kind of business you have. A sales representative is someone who showcases and sells a product or products to businesses, organizations and government agencies, rather than selling directly to consumers.

There are quite a variety of jobs available for sales representatives. They have numerous products to sell and each product requires an excellent understanding of the product, and sales representatives are expected to attend conferences and trade shows in order to keep up with products and customers' needs.

Sales representatives have distinct personalities. They are enterprising individuals that are adventurous, ambitious, assertive, extroverted, energetic, enthusiastic, confident, and optimistic. They are dominant, persuasive, and motivational. Some of them are also conventional, meaning they are thorough and conservative. The job of a sales representative can be highly variable. Many people are expected to travel, at least locally, and sometimes nationally or internationally.

WHAT DOES A SALES REPRESENTATIVE DO

A sales representative sells retail products, goods, and services to customers. They work with customers to find out what they want, create solutions and ensure a smooth sales process. Sales representative work to find new sales leads through business directories, client referrals, or visiting new or existing clients. Sales representatives may be under considerable pressure to meet sales quotas, and their income may be directly dependent on their work performance.

Skills Needed By a Sales Representative

Customer Service Skills: Sales representatives need to speak in a friendly manner to customers and potential customers, listening to what they need, and helping communicate options that may be of benefit to them and their situations.

- **Communication Skills**: Sales representatives need to describe to customers a product's different features, answer questions they might have, and communicate why having the product would be of benefit to them. Quick reply to customers' queries and politeness will build up the image of a representative and also the business.
- **Flexibility**: Sales representative may have to work long hours, nights, or weekends, therefore being flexible with their schedule is key to succeeding in this career.
- **Persistence**: Sales representative don't make every sale, and at times a customer can be rude or disrespectful. Yet, sales representative must be polite and patient. Being able to bounce back, have a positive attitude, and continue to move forward is important in this type of work.

A sales representative definitely requires extensive product knowledge of whatever he or she is selling, and is more successful when skilled at talking to people and experienced at various sales tactics. People using technical products come to trust sales representatives who can give them good advice, not only on the goods he or she is selling, but about their businesses. At some companies, sales representatives are required to learn specific sales tactics, and will even train employees on the way they want their products sold.

The Difference between Marketing and Sales

Sales and marketing are closely related but they do diverse activities in business. The sales team doesn't have any say in what the product is or who buys it – they simply take leads and convince them to buy. Employees working in sales must build close relationships with your customers and they need intelligence from marketing in order to do this.

The marketing team provides these leads by informing potential customers about your brand and product. They also use customer feedback and intelligence to decide what products to produce in the future or how to change existing products so they meet the customer needs better. You will not be effective at selling unless the people you are selling to already have some awareness about your brand or product – this is what marketing can do for you.

For a successful strategy, marketing and sales teams need to work closely together and have a unified approach. This ensures that only good-quality leads are passed to the sales team. You can use a marketing automation platform to align your marketing and sales teams to ensure they're working more efficiently towards a common goal.

Marketing a new venture

Before you succeed in marketing a new venture, you must (a) know your market. You need to gain an in-depth understanding of factors including the potential demand for your product, consumers' preferences and the strength of the competition. (b) Set your strategy (c) Create a marketing schedule and (d) avoid the common traps.

CHARACTERISTICS AND CHALLENGES

Marketing is considered to be of utmost importance for the success of new ventures. New ventures usually start off as relatively small organizations with only a handful of employees and very limited financial resources. Although some new ventures are able to acquire venture capital and thus lessen problems.

New ventures have distinct characteristics that distinguish them from larger and more established organizations. These characteristics include their newness, their small size, as well as the inherent uncertainty of the undertaking. Their markets often are characterized by high growth and turbulence.

New organizations face extensive liabilities of newness. These liabilities lead to higher failure rates of new firms compared to older ones. Majority of new firms have problems in raising capital. Resource scarcity makes small firms vulnerable, as their ability to sustain economic downtrends is limited. Most of the time, they encounter critical gaps in required skills due to lower skill diversity and disadvantages when competing with larger firms for employees. It has been observed that smallness is negatively correlated with survival rates. However, small firms also have some advantages over larger firms. In small firms processes are more flexible and communication is more direct. Thus, small firms tend to arrive at decisions faster than do their larger counterparts, and can act in a speedier fashion when discovering opportunities in the marketplace.

Newness of the Organization

New ventures are unknown to their would-be customers and other parties, which often translate into a lack of trust in their abilities and what they can offer. Hence, young firms are challenged to win customers. Before such firms even have a company identity, brand name, or track record, they must devote marketing resources to building an identity. However, such processes are often lengthy and costly. The lack of exchange relationships of new ventures is challenging not only in the context of customers, but also for other parties such as distributors and suppliers. In many industries, establishing exchange relationships can be very difficult, as access to potential partners is restricted and costly (e.g., up-front payments for distributors). As such relationships often serve as critical complementary assets; they represent substantial barriers to market entry when they cannot be attained.

As with external relationships in marketing, new ventures are challenged to establish internal structures and processes in marketing by defining new roles and tasks. However, since too much formalization can have a negative impact on response times to market changes, implementing effective and efficient internal structures and processes is a demanding task. Also, emerging firms typically lack experience in marketing which means errors in marketing planning and execution are more likely. Yet, due to resource scarcities, errors may have fatal consequences for new ventures, because they cannot afford expensive trial-and-error processes. In addition, they cannot draw on historical data in their marketing planning, making this process more challenging than it is in established firms.

Small Size of the Organization

Marketing in new ventures faces severe resource limitations in terms of finances and personnel. In general, this limits the options and the scope of strategies new ventures can pursue. For example, since new ventures are unable to finance large-scale market development efforts, they might have to target small market niches and thus miss potential first-mover advantages in the wider segment. Resource scarcity also demands a high degree of effectiveness and efficiency in the marketing efforts of young companies. Small firms must develop imaginative forms of marketing that are low-cost, but produce a strong impact on the market place (e.g., revolutionary marketing). Also, few marketing personnel means that new ventures often lack critical skills in marketing. Apart from resource limitations, smallness is usually associated with limited market presence and lack of market power. Thus, in many cases, small companies cannot achieve meaningful economies of scale and scope in marketing. It is more likely that marketing faces higher costs, because partners such as chain distributors might make use of market power to get larger margins from new firms.

Uncertainty and Instability

Due to the high degree of uncertainty and instability surrounding innovative solutions in new markets, the predictability of market data is restricted and only limited information is available for marketing planning. For example, there is little information on the nature and level of demand for new offerings. On the contrary, both depend on the strength and ingenuity of the marketing effort. Thus, critical decisions in marketing (e.g., client criteria for choice, quality/cost trade-offs) must be based on vague predictions, which leads to a higher level of trial-and-error in marketing that emerging firms are hardly able to afford. Furthermore, to be prepared for several scenarios, new ventures must keep strategic options open. However, due to resource scarcities, new firms have only limited ability to pursue several strategic options at once. Also, a revision of earlier decisions possibly disrupts the strategic guidance in marketing and causes internal instability. Because of uncertainty and instability it is likely that best practices in marketing have yet to be determined for a specific industry.

A new venture is hard pressed to win widespread acceptance for its own offering and to establish it as the dominant solution in the industry. There are several challenges in marketing that are specific to new ventures. These include the lack of an image and reputation, the lack of exchange relationships, and the lack of internal marketing structures and processes. Yet, some marketers face a multitude of challenges, which must be successfully addressed by an emerging firm these are also issues of concern in established companies, for example, when new products are launched. However, the uniqueness of marketing in new ventures can be explained by the fact that entrepreneurs face all of the identified challenges almost simultaneously, but the marketing departments of larger companies usually encounter only a rift of the challenges.

Business Plan Alignment

This is the time to ensure your marketing plan aligns with your business goals. If your business plan states that you will cover 20 villages in six months, your marketing plan has to reflect how that is going to be achieved.

Create Awareness

Creating awareness is a- must- to- do for new businesses. You cannot sell anything if no one knows you exist. Without a lot of money to spend, public relation is the best marketing investment. Perfect your description of who you are and what you do and contact business editors to let them know about your company. Create business names and pages in social media and recruit every family member and friend you have both in your phone contact list to follow you to promote your name. If you have the budget to hire a writer or freelance person, do it.

Create Partnerships

There is a saying that "no man is an island". Find businesses that sell compatible products and work out referral partnerships or joint marketing agreements for example, a Printer can partner with a Publisher and this will increase one's exposure and if the other party that has name recognition allows you, ride on that recognition while you establish your business.

Get Customers

It is obvious that getting those first customers validates one's business. Be persevering in courting them; design promotions to reward the early adopters and then ask them to champion your business with positive online reviews. Offer sales incentives to get people to try you. Once you have your customers, do everything you can to retain them. Get their feedback and use it to improve on your business. Implement loyalty programs for repeat purchases. Since they have proven that they are willing to give you their money, you need to repeat business to sustain your venture.

10 Marketing Strategies that will stimulate Business Growth

Growing a business is not easy. First, you need a viable idea. From there, you need to discover a profitable niche, define a target demographic and have something of value to sell. Whether you are peddling products, services or information, getting the word out has become increasingly burdensome. And without the right marketing strategies to fuel your growth, making a profit and staying buoyant is practically unattainable.

However, identifying the right strategies to market a business is a big undertaking. How does one get his/her message across to the right audience effectively? How do you enhance visibility and increase sales while sustaining a profit with a converting offer?

Most entrepreneurs are so busy working "in" their businesses that they fail to work "on" their businesses. As a result of dealing with the day-to-day operations of a company that includes customer hand-holding, supply-chain demands and more, most entrepreneurs often neglect to use the right marketing strategies that will help fuel their business's growth. No matter what marketing strategy one uses, if he/she does not have an effective sales funnel and optimize conversions, he/she will just be throwing money away.

What are the best marketing strategies to use?

Most businesses are faced with a challenge. There is a clear need for increased visibility to drastically improve sales. But in order to get more visibility, businesses have to spend more money. When that well runs dry, what are you supposed to do?

There is no obvious and clear answer to that question that covers all situations. But there are things that can be done today, right now, even on a shoestring budget, to reach more customers without breaking the bank. However, it all boils down to time. If you lack the money, you sure better have the time to put in the sweat equity.

Either way you slice it, as long as the fundamentals of a sound business are there and you're working tirelessly to build an authentic relationship with the consumer by sincerely trying to add value, then there are 10 go-to strategies you can use to market any business online.

1. Use social media.

Social media cannot be ignored by any serious minded entrepreneur. Some businesses have been built solely on the backs of social media because that is where all the so-called magic is happening. Social media at first can sure be intimidating. As time goes on and one builds momentum, posting on social media gets easier and easier.

Any entrepreneur that has the money could hire a social media manager. It is advisable for an entrepreneur that cannot afford a social media manager's services to be himself, be authentic, post thoughts, post products,   post anything that is relevant and useful that would help his/her audience either learn more about him/her and business, or about the industry that he/she is in.

Direct messages on platforms like Instagram and even Snapchat or Twitter should be used to reach out to other successful businesses or even to communicate with potential customers who might be looking for products and services. This is very powerful marketing.

2. Create video tutorials.

One of the most effective ways to get the world out on your business is to create video tutorials. Teach people something useful. Walk them through it. Hold their hands. Step-by-step tutorials are all the rage. The better you are at this, and the more value you provide, the quicker you can boost your visibility, and ultimately, your sales.

Today, YouTube is the second largest search engine in the world behind Google. Whenever someone wants to learn something visually, they head there. You have likely done it yourself countless times. So just ask yourself what you could teach in your business that would help consumers solve some pain point. You must not appear visually on camera, but you will likely need to be heard. You cannot ignore the visibility and reach of YouTube so get out there and start making authentic and useful videos today.

3. Start blogging now.

Sure, you could start a blog. If you do not have a blog for your business, then you need to start one immediately. But you do not just have to blog on your own blog. Most people find blogging unexciting because they lack the visibility. The truth is that your blog is going to be like a wasteland unless you know what you are doing.

But this is not just about posting your ideas on your own blog. You should start authority blogging. Use platforms to answer questions Or get out there onto LinkedIn's publishing platform. Use authority domains which have massive audiences, giving you instant and immediate reach when you post on them.

When you do blog, ensure that you blog effectively. Do not post skeletal content. Think about adding value. Do not be worried about revealing all your business secrets. Give people so much value that you instantly become an authority in their eyes. This is one of the most powerful strategies you can use to market any business.

4. Understand search engine optimization (SEO)

SEO is an area that many people are stony frightened by. Yes, SEO can be frightening. But it can also be powerful. And when you learn to leverage it and you learn SEO the right way, the sky truly is the limit. You cannot take shortcuts with SEO. Just like in business, you have to put in the work and the time if you want to see good results. Ensure that whatever it is that you are conveying is insightful, engaging, unique, and adds a tremendous amount of value.

5. Leverage influencers

Want to get the word out there and boost your visibility on social media without taking years to build the audience? Then you should certainly leverage influencers. But the key is to find the right influencer. You don't have to go with influencers with millions of followers. You could opt for micro-influencers with tens of thousands or even a hundred thousand followers.

Find the right influencer in your niche so that you are targeting the right audience. It is not just about spreading your message. It is bout spreading your message to the right consumer base. If you can do that properly, then you can likely reach a sizable audience for not much money invested when you think about the potential profit it can return.

If your sales systems and products are in place, then this makes sense. If you have an offer that is clearly converting, and it is simply about more visibility, then this is likely the right marketing strategy. Assess the situation and reach out to influencers and gauge their pricing. Do small tests and see what works, then scale.

6. Build a great lead magnet.

Effectiveness in marketing boils down to creating a great lead magnet. I've found that the right lead magnet presented to the right audience can have explosive results. The best way to do this is if you can identify the right pain points and present a solution in your lead magnet, then you're well on your way.

What problem are consumers facing in your niche? What made you get into business in the first place? Ask yourself these questions before building out your lead magnet. The better you identify the problem or pain points at the outset, the better you'll be at actually addressing that with a solution in your lead magnet.

What type of lead magnet should you build? That could either be an ebook, a cheat sheet, a checklist, a video and others. Of course, it's not just about the lead magnet. You have to have a squeeze page with sizzling sales copy to get people to drop into your funnel. But it all starts with a great lead magnet. The better it is, the more effective you'll be at reaching your audience.

7. Use Facebook ads with re-targeting.

Facebook ads is one of the most powerful methods one can use to market just about anything these days. With Facebook, one can reach a very specific audience and can also do it very easily and efficiently. One can target among others by affiliate, interest, age, relationships status geographic location. Getting great results here is not just about click-traffic. You have to focus on conversions and re-targeting through pixels. If you do not know how to install the Facebook Pixel on your site, then you absolutely must learn how to do this right now. Even if you are not running Facebook ads, you can build your audience with a pixel.

Pixels track everyone who comes to your site, and you can build custom audiences around them. For example, if you post content about how to learn to drive a semi-truck, and you track visitors with pixels, you can then market truck driving certification to people who have already shown an interest in that already because they visited that specific page. And your conversions will skyrocket.

8. Use LinkedIn the right way.

LinkedIn is one of the social media sites that most people under use the facilities or services that it provides. Do you have a video on your LinkedIn profile? Did you know that you can easily add one? Why not take the time to introduce yourself and your business. Link that to your profile description. This is an easy way to passively market your business, and when it's done right, it can lead to shocking results. You can do this to other social media site.

If you have lots of connections on LinkedIn and you are not really posting on there, start immediately. You can reach a large audience, especially when your posts go viral. This is a great place to convey the entrepreneurial journey. Talk about your challenges and tell stories. The more effective your stories, the larger your potential reach when you go viral. You can also reach out to other businesses and collaborate with like-minded entrepreneurs on LinkedIn.

9. Create an affiliate program.

Most people do not understand the power of affiliate marketing. Affiliates can stimulate growth. Approaching the right partners is not always that easy. For bigger affiliate to take one seriously there must be a good conversion. It is tricky to navigating the affiliate (associate) minefield. It takes persistence to make it through. Most people get discouraged after a few setbacks, but one cannot allow emotions to get in the way when it comes to associate. It is advisable to build an affiliate program and start reaching out to potential affiliate who can be of great assistance.

10. Use Email Marketing Sequences

Email marketing sequence is part of a good sales funnel. They are automated messages that go out to users once they subscribe to one's list. Email sequence can be used to build a relationship with the subscriber. Be authentic, transparent and convey your journey.

Use the email responses and clicks to fragment your list. For example, if someone clicks on a specific link, they have clearly shown an interest in something. Tag that subscriber to market to them later. If someone buys, tag them as a buyer. Identifying your buyers and the interests of your subscribers is enormous for segmenting.

Quick Takeaways:

- At a fundamental level, marketing is the process of understanding your customers, and building and maintaining relationships with them.
- Marketing is the key to an organization's success, regardless of its size.
- There are several types and sub-types of marketing, digital and offline. You should determine and pursue the ones that work best for you.
- Marketing and Sales teams need to have a unified approach. Automation helps them work towards the same goals.

CHAPTER SIX

CAPITAL REQUIREMENT

Capital is a term for financial possessions (assets), such as funds held in deposit accounts and/or funds obtained from special financing sources. Capital can also be associated with capital assets of a company that requires significant amounts of capital to finance or expand. Capital can be held through financial assets or raised from debt or equity financing. Capital assets are assets of a business found on either the current or long-term portion of the balance sheet. Capital assets can include cash, cash equivalents, and marketable securities as well as manufacturing equipment, production facilities, and storage facilities.

Capital is used to provide ongoing production of goods and services for creating profit. Companies use capital to invest in all kinds of things for the purpose of creating value for a firm. Labor and building expansions can be two areas where capital is often allocated. By investing through the use of capital, a business or individual directs their money toward investments that earn a higher return than the capital's costs.

From a financial capital economics perspective, capital is a key part of running a business and growing an economy. Companies have capital structures that include debt capital, equity capital, and working capital for daily expenditures. Individuals hold capital and capital assets as part of their net worth. How individuals and companies finance their working capital and invest their obtained capital is critical for growth and return on investment. Capital is typically cash or liquid assets held or obtained for expenditures. In general, capital can be a measurement of wealth and also a resource that provides for increasing wealth through direct investment or capital project investments.

The financial capital economics definition can be analyzed by economists to understand how capital in the economy is influencing economic growth. Economists watch several metrics of capital including personal income and personal consumption from the Commerce Department's Personal Income and Outlays reports as well as investment found in the quarterly Gross Domestic Product report.

Business Capital Structure

Businesses need a substantial amount of capital to operate and create profitable returns. Businesses typically focus on three types of business capital: working capital, equity capital, and debt capital. In general, business capital is a core part of running a business and financing capital intensive assets.

Balance sheet analysis is central to the review and assessment of business capital. Split between assets, liabilities, and equity, a company's balance sheet provides for metric analysis of a capital structure. Debt financing provides a cash capital asset that must be repaid over time through scheduled liabilities. Equity financing provides cash capital that is also reported in the equity portion of the balance sheet with an expectation of return for the investing shareholders. Debt capital typically comes with lower relative rates of return alongside strict provisions for repayment. Some of the key metrics for analyzing business capital include weighted average cost of capital, debt to equity, debt to capital, and return on equity.

It is worthy to note that:

- Capital is a term for financial assets, such as funds held in deposit accounts and funds obtained from special financing sources.
- Financing capital usually comes with a cost.
- The four major types of capital include debt, equity, trading, and working capital.
- Companies must decide which types of capital financing to use as parts of their capital structure.

Types of Capital

Types of capital are: **Debt Capital, Equity Capital, Working Capital and Trading Capital**

Debt Capital

A business can acquire capital through the assumption of debt. Debt capital can be obtained through private or government sources. Sources of capital can include friends, family, financial institutions, online lenders, credit card companies, insurance companies, and federal loan programs.

Individuals and companies must typically have an active credit history to obtain debt capital. Debt capital requires regular repayment with interest. Interest varies depending on the type of capital obtained and the borrower's credit history.

Equity Capital

Equity capital can come in several forms. Typically distinctions are made between private equity, public equity, and real estate equity. Private and public equity will usually be structured in the form of shares. Public equity capital raises occur when a company lists on a public market exchange and receives equity capital from shareholders. Private equity is not raised in the public markets. Private equity usually comes from selected investors or owners

Working Capital

Working capital includes a company's most liquid capital assets available for fulfilling daily obligations. It is calculated on a regular basis through the following two assessments:

Current Assets – Current Liabilities

Accounts Receivable + Inventory – Accounts Payable

Working capital measures a company's short-term liquidity, more specifically, its ability to cover its debts, accounts payable, and other obligations that are due within one year.

Trading Capital

Trading capital may be held by individuals or firms who place a large number of trades on a daily basis. Trading capital refers to the amount of money allotted to buy and sell various securities.

Investors may attempt to add to their trading capital by employing a variety of trade optimization methods. These methods attempt to make the best use of capital by determining the ideal percentage of funds to invest with each trade. In particular, to be successful, it is important for traders to determine the optimal cash reserves required for their investing strategies.

Is Capital Money?

It is worthy to note that capital is money. However, for financial and business purposes capital is typically viewed from an operational and investment perspective. Capital usually comes with a cost. For debt capital, this is the cost of interest required in repayment. For equity capital, this is the cost of distributions made to shareholders. Overall, capital is deployed to help shape a company's development and growth.

Related Terms

Corporate Capital: Corporate capital is the mix of assets or resources a company can draw on as a result of debt and equity financing.

Private Equity: Private equity is a non-publicly traded source of capital from investors who seek to invest or acquire equity ownership in a company

Fixed Capital: Fixed capital includes the assets, such as property, plant, and equipment that are needed to start up and conduct business, even at a minimal stage.

Financial Statements: Financial statements are written records that convey the business activities and the financial performances of a company. Financial statements include the balance sheet, income statement, and cash flow statement.

Return on Invested Capital: Return on invested capital (ROIC) is a way to assess a company's efficiency at allocating the capital under its control to profitable investments.

Financial Structure: Financial structure refers to the mix of debt and equity that a company uses to finance its operations.

Start up Business *Capital*

Start-up capital is the fund a business owner will need to finance the production of a good and the sale of that good.

Small Business *capital requirement*

Before an entrepreneur succeeds in floating or starting up a business, there must be a capital. The three primary factors that determine how much working *capital* the entrepreneur will need to start up a *small business* are: business type, operating cycle, and management goals. The *capital requirement* is the sum of funds that a *company* needs to achieve its goals. This means the total amount of money a small *business* needs for a start up.

For a small business, capital simply is money. This is the financing for a small business or the money used to operate and buy assets. Capital here is the money businesses use for financing their operations. The cost of capital is simply the rent, or interest rate, it costs the business to obtain financing.

Working capital requirement for a small business

Working capital requirement includes wages, taxes and accounts payable. Current Assets divided by current liabilities. Your current ratio helps you determine if you have enough working capital to meet your short-term financial obligations

A capital requirement (also known as regulatory capital or capital adequacy)

This is the amount of capital a <u>bank</u> or other financial institution has to have as required by its financial supervisory body. This is usually expressed as a capital adequacy ratio of equity as a percentage of risk-weighted assets. These requirements are put into place to ensure that these institutions do not take on excess leverage and risk becoming bankrupt. Capital requirements govern the ratio of equity to debt, recorded on the liabilities and equity side of a firm's balance sheet. They should not be confused with reserve requirements, which govern the assets side of a bank's balance sheet—in particular, the proportion of assets it must hold in cash or highly-liquid assets. Capital is a source of funds not a use of funds.

A key part of bank regulation is to make sure that firms operating in the industry are prudently managed. The aim is to protect the firms themselves, their customers, the government (which is liable for the cost of deposit insurance in the event of a bank failure) and the economy, by establishing rules to make sure that these institutions hold enough capital to ensure continuation of a safe and efficient market and are able to withstand any foreseeable problems.

Supplementary capital: this comprises undisclosed reserves, revaluation reserves, general provisions, hybrid instruments and subordinated term debt.

Undisclosed reserves: these are where a bank has made a profit but this has not appeared in normal retained profits or in general reserves.

A revaluation reserve: this is a reserve created when a company has an asset revalued and an increase in value is brought to account. A simple example may be where a bank owns the land and building of its headquarters and bought them for 200 naira a century ago. A current revaluation is very likely to show a large increase in value. The increase would be added to a revaluation reserve.

A general provision: this is created when a company is aware that a loss has occurred, but is not certain of the exact nature of that loss.

Hybrid debt capital instruments:

These consist of instruments which combine certain characteristics of equity as well as debt. They can be included in supplementary capital if they are able to support losses on an ongoing basis without triggering liquidation. Sometimes, it includes instruments which are initially issued with interest obligation (e.g. debentures) but the same can later be converted into capital.

The Basics of Capital Requirements

Capital requirements are standardized regulations in place for banks and other depository institutions that determine how much liquid capital (that is, easily sold securities) must be held *vis-a-vis* a certain level of their assets.

Regulatory capital standards are set by regulatory agencies. Regulators in each country have some discretion on how they implement capital requirements in their jurisdiction.

Capital requirements are set to ensure that banks and depository institutions' holdings are not dominated by investments that increase the risk of default. They also ensure that banks and depository institutions have enough capital to sustain operating losses (OL) while still honoring withdrawals.

Capital Requirements: Benefits and Drawbacks
Capital requirements aim not only to keep banks solvent but, by extension, to keep the entire financial system on a safe footing. In an era of national and international finance, no bank is an island as regulatory advocates note—a shock to one can affect many. So, all the more reason for stringent standards that can be applied consistently and used to compare the different soundness of institutions.

Still, capital requirements have their critics. They charge that higher capital requirements have the potential to reduce bank risk-taking and competition in the financial sector (on the basis that regulations always prove costlier to smaller institutions than to larger ones). By mandating banks to keep a certain percentage of assets liquid, the requirements can inhibit the institutions' ability to invest and make money—and thus extend credit to customers. Maintaining certain levels of capital can increase their costs, which in turn increases costs for borrowing or other services for consumers.

A capital buffer refers to extra capital required by regulators for financial institutions to ensure a more resilient global banking system.

Core capital is the minimum amount of capital that a bank must have on hand in order to comply with Federal Home Loan Bank regulations.

It is worthy to note that:

- Capital requirements are regulatory standards for banks that determine how much liquid capital (easily sold assets) they must keep on hand, concerning their overall holdings.
- Express as a ratio the capital requirements are based on the weighted risk of the banks' different assets.
- Capital requirements are often tightened after an economic recession, stock market crash, or another type of financial crisis.

CHAPTER SEVEN

JOB CREATION

Job creation can be seen as the process by which the number of jobs in an economy increases. It often refers to as government policies intended to reduce unemployment. Job creation can take a variety of forms. For example, the Government may decide to lower taxes and reduce regulations to make hiring less expensive. The Government may hire workers directly to clean or beautify the environment, to build a road etc

Job creation can also be seen as the employment growth contributed by establishments that expand or start up while job destruction is employment decline resulting from establishments end of contract or shut down. The sum of job creation and job destruction is the net change in employment.

Government can create Employment by increasing irrigation facilities. For example, without irrigation only a single crop can be grown in most agricultural fields and this means less working opportunities but if irrigation is provided, more crops can be grown on the same field and this means employment for more people. Also, when credit facilities are made available to entrepreneurs, there will be creation of more business lines and this will mean more employment openings.

Job creation and economic growth are related. The more people work, the more the economy becomes stable. Economic stability is needed for people to make big investments in themselves and family members.

Steps that can be taken to create more employment

(i) **Increase in irrigation facilities** :- Without irrigation only a single crop is grown in most agricultural fields. It means less working opportunities, but if irrigation is provided two or three crops can be grown on the same field. So more people will be employed.
(ii) **Improved Roads and Transportation** :- If village roads are better built,

good transportation facilities are provided then, surplus produce could be sold in city market. This would fetch more income.

(iii) **Provide them easy loan** :- If people are provided easy bank loans then they could start small business which will make them self dependent.

Self employment

A self-employed job either part-time, full-time, remote, or in person, creative or not can get one to his goals.

The European Commission (2010) defines a self-employed person as someone: "pursuing a gainful activity for their own account, under the conditions lay down by national law". In the exercise of such an activity, the personal element is of special importance and such exercise always involves a large measure of independence in the accomplishment of the professional activities. In other words, a self employed is that individual who does not provide services or labour for commercial enterprise to receive wages or remuneration rather he works for himself under the supervision of nobody and bear the risk and enjoy the gains or benefits and he can also make and grow his own opportunities. This is in contrast to an employee who provides services or labuor for the commercial enterprise, and who receives wages or remuneration directly from the enterprise. An employee is subordinate to and dependent on an employer.

Becoming a self-employed contractor has many advantages. Whether you are planning to leave your current job or seeking a way to make additional income, self-employment often provides professionals with greater freedom and flexibility than one may experience working directly for an employer. In addition to setting your own rates and hours, self-employed jobs give you the opportunity to work as little or as much as you need. Working for self employment can be best for parents who want to spend more time at home, students who need to work around a class schedule or anyone who wants to explore entrepreneurship.

Starting your own business, being the boss, and calling the shots are all very attractive to anyone with an entrepreneurial urge. It can also be one of the easiest ways to transition from full-time employment to running your own business, provided you have solid skills and experience in your profession.

However, as the saying goes that anything that has advantages, has its own disadvantages, self-employment has its challenges. You should fully understand and prepare for all aspects of entrepreneurship in order to avoid unpleasant surprises down the road. Here are what you need to know to start and build a successful business as a self-employed:

(a) Be Sure You Want to Be Self-Employed
(b) Get Financing in Place Beforehand.
(c) Create a Business Plan.
(d) Name, Register, and Insure Your Contracting Business.
(e) Market Your Business.
(f) Be Your Own Accountant, for Starters.

Be Sure You Want to Be Self-Employed

What will determine the value of a self-employed job is whether or not it is right for you. Not everyone is suited to be their own boss. Before you make this decision, ask yourself two important questions: Does self-employment suit your life circumstances and is your personality suited to self-employment?

If you have a well-paid job with benefits and reasonable job satisfaction, it may not be necessary to become self-employed, no matter your desire to become an entrepreneur. Also, organizing vacations, making major purchases, and planning retirement are much easier when you have a steady paycheck and regular working hours, especially if you are breadwinner. Thorough examination of your lifestyle, financial situation, and future retirement goals are very important. Discuss them with your family before making the leap to self-employment.

Being your own boss means all the responsibilities for the success of your business rest on your shoulders. If your personality is such that dealing with the uncertainties of self-employment is likely to cause you a great deal of stress and anxiety, then being an entrepreneur is probably not for you.

Get Financing in Place Beforehand

How much capital (if any) will you need for renting of shop, equipment, etc.? Capital financing may not be an issue for a computer consultant who can start a home-based consulting business with only a laptop and mobile phone. In addition to capital financing, you will need to cover business and personal expenses until your business generates income, Even if you already have clients when you start the business, it may be months before you get paid for the completion of your first project.

Before you make the move to become a freelancer, perform a complete review of your finances and estimate your needs as closely as possible, then (if needed) consider possible sources of financing, such as family, friends, or business loans from financial institutions (though it is practically difficult to get financing for a new business from a bank unless you have sufficient collateral in the form of personal assets).

If financing is required and you intend to seek loans or capital investment from equity investors, then you will need to have a comprehensive outline of your financial requirements as part of your business plan.

Create a Business Plan

Do you need a business plan? If, for example, you are fortunate enough that you can leave your current full-time job and be immediately rehired as a contractor, or are starting a business with clients already in place and no financing requirements, then perhaps not.

Name, Register, and Insure Your Contracting Business

Before you open your doors and start taking on any clients as a contractor, you will need to:

During the startup phase of your business, you can save money on accounting fees by using free time to organize your books, create systems for invoicing your customers, and learn basic accounting. Or better still there are Accounting software that can greatly simplify your bookkeeping chores. Many of the new cloud-based accounting software packages such as FreshBooks and Zoho offer ideal starter packages for self-employed contractors that include invoicing, expense tracking, simple reporting, and mobile applications. If you are reluctant to do your own bookkeeping, you can always hire a bookkeeper or accountant to perform these duties once you become busy with clients.

Be Professional at All Times

As a professional librarian, look and act the part at all times. Potential customers who do not know you will be turned off by inappropriate dress or behavior on your part. Being professional also means answering the phone properly, using voicemail, and responding promptly to messages or emails. In today's world of online reviews and social media, developing a reputation for poor customer service can quickly become disastrous for your business. If you intend to conduct business from home and need to meet with clients, make sure you have a separate, properly equipped and furnished home office space.

Build Your Reputation with Best Practices

The ideal client is one you keep for the life of your business. To do so, you need to rise above the competition by:

- Developing a reputation for honesty and integrity
- Under-promising and over-delivering
- Making good on all mistakes
- Treating every client as special and finding ways to thank them regularly

Over-extending yourself and making impossible promises is a sure way to lose customers in the long term.

Avoid Potential Tax Issues by Having Multiple Clients

If your business is growing and you are finding that there are not enough hours in the day, Outsourcing some of these secondary tasks can free up more time to focus on your core business activities. Consider sub-contracting some of your non-core tasks like: web designing or management of your business social media postings, deliver of products to customers, making of traveling arrangements, keeping of books and doing taxes etc.

Some of your reliable family members can help in performing some of these duties that may come with some tax benefits.

Be Sure You are Ready Before You Expand

Many successful contracting businesses reach a point where further expansion would require hiring additional people to handle the increased workload. Hiring or contracting additional personnel is a difficult decision, and many self-employed contractors prefer to remain solo for a number of reasons such as:

- The more specialized your business, the more difficult it may be to find qualified people.
- Advertising, vetting resumes, and interviewing is very time-consuming. Once you make your hires, training, supervision, and related paperwork will require more of your time.
- Unless additional personnel generate more income than the cost of their employment, your profits will not increase.
- The reputation of your business may suffer if whoever you hire does not perform at the expected level.

Many contractors find it easier and less stressful to stay small, keep their workload within manageable limits, and maintain a positive cash flow by controlling business costs. On the other hand, if your ambition is to build a larger business and you have the time and energy to put into expansion then, by all means, take the push.

Maintain a well-balanced, lifestyle

Try not to let your business become your entire life—a well-balanced, healthy lifestyle includes a proper diet, exercise, and time for personal relationships with family and friends. Putting all your time and energy into your business to earn money for retirement or other purposes is pointless if it leads to declining physical or mental health.

Opportunities for self employment

Interested in working for yourself and building a business as a solopreneur? There are more opportunities than ever for individuals to make a solid living while being self-employed. No matter one's skills, interests or experience, there is sure to be a type of self-employment that is well suited to one's needs. It is possible to be an employee and the same time self-employed. This could be made possible when for example, one work for an employer part time and at the same time run his own business part time.

There are several self-employed jobs available today. Jobs like: Graphic designer, Photographer, Writer, Social media specialist, Developer, etc.

Graphic designer: Before one goes into Graphic designing, he should have an understanding of design and colour theory and be skilled at using design software programs because Graphic designers use software to create customized graphics for websites, advertisements, and other digital and printed materials. A graphic designer can offer services on a freelance or contractual basis. For example, he can design logos, websites or branding elements for businesses. They may help companies develop their logos and other branding collateral.

Photography: this is the act of using cameras and photography equipment to take pictures of people, places and objects for organizations or individuals. Photographers usually specialize in one or more areas, such as weddings, photojournalism, wildlife and more. In most cases, photographers need to supply their own equipment. Before one goes into photography, he should be highly skilled in manual digital photography and have a strong background in photo editing and photo editing software.

A Writer: before one becomes a successful writer he should have excellent grammar and spelling skills, and a background in journalism, creative writing or mass communication. A freelance writer is someone who writes articles, advertising copy, scripts, books and other materials for individuals or organizations. They may also be required to research topics and edit their own work.

Social media specialist: this is an important way for businesses to connect with ordinary people, without having to go through all channels. If you spend a lot of time on social media – Facebook, Twitter, Snapchat, Instagram, YouTube or other outlets, you may be able to find some clients who are in need of a social media consultant. If you know how to promote events, products, and even concepts, using social media, then this can be the perfect business for you. What started out as a social game just a few years ago is rapidly becoming important in the business community. It is a way to market businesses, products, and services.

Social media specialist is an individual that has an in-depth knowledge of social media marketing, how to drive organic and paid social media engagement and the ability to interpret analytics, set goals and report on performance can be a Social media specialist. A specialist uses marketing strategies to build and manage the following on platforms such as Facebook, Instagram, Twitter, YouTube and more. Typically, they work on behalf of organizations or public figures.

Virtual Assistant Service: If you want to work from home and enjoy a fairly flexible schedule, you could work with business owners as a virtual assistant. Virtual assistant can handle a variety of tasks, from social media to inbox management. Choose a specialty or offer a wide array of services to clients.

Web design: almost everybody wants to start a website of some type, but most people lack the skills to make it happen. If you know how to build even simple websites for upstart businesses that have limited budgets and later turn that into a full-fledged business. If nothing else, you can prepare simple websites. As your business grows and your skill level and your client base increases, you can begin doing more complicated websites for higher fees.

Whether you are a video producer, web designer, or social media consultant, you may be able to sell your freelancing skills on a site where people hire talented professionals for their creative needs.

Developer: before a person becomes a developer, such a person should be knowledgeable in a variety of programming languages. Some clients may need developers who are especially skilled in one type of language or database representation. A developer uses coding languages to design, install, test and maintain software systems, websites and applications.

Tutoring Service: a library and Information graduate might consider starting his own tutoring services in librarianship where he will work with students one-on-one. Tutors visit students at their homes or at another location such as library, school or town hall, to conduct lessons and assist students in improving their academic performances. Some tutors work virtually, meeting with students via video chat software. You can market your tutoring business just by creating a professional-looking flyer, and distributing it to schools.

For success in tutoring, basic interpersonal communication skills are a must. A tutor must excel in the subject area that he tutors, and must also be motivational and encouraging.

Business Consultant

Most businesses need specific help either with an established area of the business or in taking on an entirely new function. A consultant can come in and help them do just that. The advantage is that the consultant will be coming in as a fee-based independent contractor, rather than as an employee in need of a permanent salary and benefits.

One of the best ways to do this is by offering related services. Identify your specialization, then figure out ways that you can help various businesses move forward, and you will have created a consulting niche for yourself.

Business consultants work with companies to help improve performance in a specific area. For example, some business consultants specialize in fields like revenue growth, human resources, management, and sales operations; also if you have significant marketing experience, you can act as a marketing consultant for a retail operation, a computer software company, or an e-commerce business.

A business consultant must be highly skilled and experienced in the area he provides expertise and also should have good communication and presentation skills and know how to measure and report performance in his field.

Videographer

An entire closet industry in the video space has developed with the arrival of YouTube. If you have been creating your own videos, such as music videos, how-to videos, or just-for-fun videos, you may be able to sell your services to the general public. Small businesses are looking for custom videos put on their websites, to broadcast through social media, and even to include in emails. Videos provide a better way to reach prospective customers who are either primarily visual learners, or people who simply do not have time to read a lengthy article or webpage.

A videographer uses filming equipment to capture videos for advertising, marketing or educational purposes. They also use editing software to create professional-quality video recording. He must be well-versed in shooting, directing and editing video. In most cases, he must try to provide his own camera and other necessary equipment.

Career coach

A career coach is someone who helps clients to identify their professional goals, develop new skills and plan their future career path. He can also help clients in locating new job opportunities and prepare them for interviews and events. A career coach must be familiar with the job market in his area of expertise, have excellent active listening skills and should be well-versed in leadership and business success strategies.

Transcriptionist

Transcriptionists listen to live or recorded speech and transcribe it into text using proper grammar and language rules. They may work directly for businesses or contract with a transcription service. Transcriptionist is an active listener who is able to type quickly and accurately. He has a comprehensive understanding or spelling and grammar.

EBook Sales

A librarian with relevant expertise in any aspect of librarianship for example, cataloguing could also sell his knowledge in the form of ebooks. He can self-publish his own work and then sell it on his own site or on existing platforms like Amazon.

Conclusion

Being self employed brings the benefits of freedom but the key success is to be constant in whatever thing you are into when you are self employed.

The above listed are some of the self-employed job ideas. There are many more opportunities available. Whether you are interested in eventually launching your own company or you want to make a little extra income outside of regular employment, there are plenty of self-employed jobs for job seekers with nearly any educational background. Each business idea on the above list will cost very little amount of money to enter, and the benefits could reach way further than you can imagine.

The chapter will be summarizing with the following tips:

Dream Big: Maybe you are starting down this path as a part-time way to make money fast. But perhaps it could grow into the career you have been looking for all your life, allowing you to not only have money but also have enough money to save and eventually create passive income.

Be Persistent: Getting to that point is the gift that keeps on giving. Some of the ideas on this list can earn for you while you are sleeping, traveling, reading, you get the idea. But it could take years of hard work and perseverance. Put in the work to make it happen.

Fix your finances: If you want to keep your personal and business finances separate, I recommend getting a separate business credit card and opening a separate checking account. This will allow you to keep business money by itself and then pay yourself a "salary" into your personal account.

Keep hustling: Whether you are looking for a long-term career or a side hustles to get you through the season, it is commendable! The next step is getting out there and making it happen. Look at your skills, check your interests, and give one of the ideas on the list a try. It's worth it

CHAPTER 8

Rebranding and Repositioning of the library/librarian

Library and Information Science has come a long way, the services of librarians are increasingly demanded across disciplines and institutions. Their work environment is becoming increasingly complex- with constant change in the organizational, technological and information environment and this calls for lifting the image of the library. For librarians to meet up with the high demands placed on their products (services) there should be a little fee attachment to the services they render to their clienteles. This will in a way raise the value of library services and also avoid the general saying that free commodities are not being handled with care since it can always be replaced without stress.

For a library to remain modern, relevant and competitive there should be a call for rebranding and this will indicate that the library and its services are up to date.

A rebrand is not an easy switch where one can wake up one day with a new emblem and business goes on as usual. Rebranding is not done in a day rather it is a gradual process it takes so much time and money. For example, you cannot suddenly dump a new brand on the business one day and expect people to use it the next day without their observing and scrutinizing.

Rebranding contemporary is a sizzling topic in the world of librarianship. Rebranding a library, or a service, or an organization, is a very delicate business – especially if you are changing the physical space along with the name and visual identity. This means: before rebranding is rightfully done, it has to be more than a name-change. It should be all encompassing, representing a change of ethos, style, or priorities. Rebranding takes so much time and money but it is worth it when handled well. In this 21th century, library rebranding should be a welcome development because the old branding is no longer effective in communicating the priorities and services of the institution; because these priorities and services have changed.

Rebranding is a marketing strategy in which a new name, term, symbol, design, concept or combination thereof is created for an established brand with the intention of developing a new, differentiated identity in the minds of consumers, investors, competitors, and other stakeholders. Branding is the term used to describe the overall design and promotion of a company, its products and services while Rebranding is the term used to describe taking an existing brand and changing or altering its message and design elements. This includes updating your website, social media and third-party sites with your new logo, slogan, imagery, content text, and so on. **Wikipedia**

In other words, Library rebranding is a strategy of giving a new name, representation, or change in plan from what the library is already known for. The idea behind rebranding is to create a different identity from its competitors, in the market. We need to rebrand the library by redefining our relevance in the modern information landscape.

Before a new brand is finally flagged out, there should be feedback from library stakeholders, employees and clienteles using a survey to ask what they like, what could be improved on and what they would change about the current branding. Similarly, at different rebranding stages, **invitation is made seeking for opinions and input.** Gathering insights will ensure that all members of the organization feel included and are on the same page, and **all necessary perspectives considered**.

Once everything is implemented, a **rebrand communication plan now provides an effective way to introduce it to the world** at large. One of the best ways of doing this is to add a blog post or news item explaining the change. Another is to intermittently share social media posts reminding customers of a new brand. Also, fliers, hand bills, notice boards etc can be used. When telling the story of a new brand, emphases should be laid on how the **changes made will improve the experience** of existing customers.

One of ways the name 'librarian'will get branded is by adoption of entrepreneurial skills for a fee-based service. In such a setting, the librarian can be called an 'info-preneur', 'knowledge entrepreneur', or 'entrepreneuria librarian' bibliognost, custodian, administrator, bibliothecary, cataloger, bibliothec, bibliosoph, keeper, caretaker, curator and officer in charge of the library.

By adopting entrepreneurial skills, the quality of services need to be raised by looking at what makes entrepreneurs thrive in their circle and bringing such secrets into the library circle.

The need to adopt entrepreneurial skills in library practices so as to enhance the traditional library practice in Nigeria has helped entrepreneurship in gaining grounds in library profession especially in the University curriculum where students are taught entrepreneurial skills and the library profession. There is a wake-up call for librarians to embrace these skills and apply them not only in their private business ventures, but also in their routine job as service providers in the library environment. Beyond entrepreneurial skills adoption by librarians for their personal practices, there is a need for librarians to apply such skills in corporate librarianship whereby thinking and acting like entrepreneurs; applying the same skills that entrepreneurs use in their business, into library businesses in a bid to meet the need of the clients in the contemporary age of business-mindedness and corporate branding. This is to say that the skills that make entrepreneurs thrive could be adopted into library practices in order to lift the image of the library and also, for librarians to see their work as their own business.

Entrepreneurial skills have been identified by Torren (2010) as very crucial for people that want to thrive in the business world to become successful. Five points identified by Torren were (i) decision making, (ii) peoples skill (iii) planning, (iv) sales, and (v) communication. Torren stated that: "In today's world, if you want to be a successful entrepreneur, there is certainly an "evolutionary" process that must be undertaken. This is to say that for an entrepreneur not to be left behind, there are skills that must be acquired and work upon in order to thrive in today's business world.

The traditional library practices have been known for provision of information to library users within the library building and these services are void of certain skills that could boost the services. The initiation of such skills is meant to move library services to a different shift. This paradigm shift is what has brought library profession to a limelight. The adaption of information and communication technology (ICT) into library system has helped librarians in gaining necessary skills that will help them in meeting the contemporary library users' needs without wasting much of their time. With the introduction of Online Public Access Catalogue (OPAC), library users can access same book and sieve the bibliographical details at the same time. With the advent of library application software, a user can borrow a book just with a click making circulation services a lot easier and hence, obeys Ranganathan's fourth law of library science (save the time of the user).

These days, seminars and workshops are held, exposing librarians to certain managerial, communication and entrepreneurial skills. The aspect of communication handles issues like teaching library personnel how to attend to users and see them as customers which they are. Unlike those days that librarians hardly wore smiles on their faces so as not to distract users nor create an environment for chats and noise. Everybody got busy, both librarians and users – doing their things till closing time. In the same line, Eke-Okpala and Ihejirika (2012) observed that Librarians want to be pushed to carry out their duties; they do not see the need to render services as if it is their own business. Once they collect their salary for the month, they are good to go instead of attempting building on their skills and take the responsibility of the success or failure of their organization

For library profession to attain greater height there is a need for librarians in the traditional library settings; to take the business mentality to the library service sector and place the library on the competitive as a service-rendering organization.

Differences between Rebranding and Repositioning

For brands that want to shed previously negative image or that are facing increased competitive pressure, rebranding is very necessary. Rebranding and repositioning are intertwined. Rebranding makes way for repositioning. Without rebranding, repositioning will not be as effective. Re-branding is not merely a change of identity as some scholars may posit. It is an entire strategy that attempts to achieve the goals of repositioning. It typically includes changing most or all of the brand identity elements. The identity change may also be accompanied by brand repositioning.

However, a brand can be repositioned without changing its identity. Repositioning focuses on changing what clienteles link with the brand and sometimes competing brand. This usually has to do with a change in the brand's promise and personality. And sometimes the identity itself is updated or refreshed to reinforce the change in the brand's positioning. However, most brand repositioning projects do not result in completely changed identities. That is, usually the brand name does not change. Positioning is a goal – a place you want to end up your customer's mind while Branding is the strategy to get there. Take for instance, if a lady chooses to rebrand herself, she loses weight, dyes her hair, fixes eye lashes, dresses differently, and changes her name, but acts exactly the same way no behavioral change – is it really re-positioning? The answer is a capital "NO".

If a person repositions himself, he changes his values, attitude, personality or behavior. Any combination of these changes can occur together or separately.

SOME BENEFITS OF REBRANDING

1. Connect With a New Audience

One of the advantages of looking new and different is the ability to reach new customers. When you focus on new aspects of your business and promote them correctly, people will take notice. Rebranding can offer the stimulation your business needs to create new growth in an ever-evolving market.

2. Set Yourself Apart From Your Competitors

As you grow your business, your capabilities may begin to directly contend with those of your industry competitors. Rebranding can be the most effective way to set your company's offers and approach apart. Differentiating your brand shows potential clients that your services are unique—and that you are the experts. Rebranding your company to have its own voice, look, and feel will help establish your business as an industry leader with a personality that appeals to your audience.

3. Stay Current

Rebranding has one simple goal: to keep your brand current. Design trends play a major role in how potential or current customers perceive your company and all it has to offer. Ensuring that your look is always ahead of the curve shows your customers that you pay attention to the trends within your industry.

4. Reflect New Goals, Products, Offers, or Values

It is hard to showcase how your company has grown when your brand does not reflect it. If you have expanded to offer new products, grown to include more services, or set new goals for your business, then rebranding is a great way to show that your business is evolving.

5. Boost Your Bottom Line

The benefits of rebranding will not only impact your overall inbound strategy, but they will make your company more profitable. Reaching new potential clients, standing out from your competitors, showcasing your expertise, and expanding the influence and reach of your products and services are all effective ways to increase your profits just by giving your brand a new look.

The Image of Librarians

According to Shamel (2002), the perception of who librarians are and what they do is often based upon what library workers look like, what they say, and what they do. Library work is service work. Information professionals offer service. Library has an identity, an identity created by the staff contact with the users. Our main product that we offer as librarians is service, and the way we deliver this service determines how we are judged by people we come in contact with

Librarianship is a people profession; the importance of a librarian cannot be over emphasized. Students, teachers, and even administrators need current information. A *librarian* is a person who works professionally in a library, providing access to information and sometimes social or technical programming to users. In addition, *librarians* provide instruction on information literacy to users. This is to say that: a librarian's job is to connect people with the information they are seeking, in whatever format. All library jobs have a central purpose: to help people access and use information, for education, for work, or for pleasure. In a nut shell, librarians are known for selecting, developing, cataloguing and classifying library resources, answering readers' enquiries, using library systems and specialist computer applications, management of staff, including recruitment, training and/or supervisory duties. Librarians throw light on reference books and help find the best online databases to meet everyone's needs. They search for new acquisitions and are skilled at researching online and in print

A good librarian possesses the following qualities: love of knowledge and learning, desire to work around people, love of books, broad overall knowledge of life and the world, strong organizational skills, good with numbers, sociable and principled.

The quality of services and the public's impression of the library depends on the librarians. The duties of a library staff should go beyond the users' earliest experience in school libraries such as: shelving of books, checking books in and out, reading the paper, and occasionally chatting with a clientele. They hear library staff enforcing the rules like: "You must sign up to use the Internet," "Please keep your voices down," "Do not shelve consulted books," or, "This is due back in 2 weeks or you will have to pay a fine." All of these tell people what "librarians" do. Customers who are aware of librarians and library services find them to be motivated and well-intentioned, but incompetent and passive. With these impressions in place, it will be difficult for the general public to see the value that an information professional could bring to sophisticated information management challenges.

The negative image of actual librarians includes passivity, incompetence, bureaucratic tendencies, and insufficient education or subject knowledge for the job. On the credit side, real-life librarians were thought to possess service motivation, a sense of duty, and a desire to help others especially in this era of digitization and information explosion.

Employers and library potential customers find next to nothing in their own literature about who librarians are and what they do. For this reason, librarians should give a good image of themselves by making sure that the schools that train business managers and professionals have a lot to say about the role of a librarian or information professional in achieving corporate success.

Librarians should be offered some of the tools needed to promote the value of library services for example; there should be a number of publications targeting the information industry, sections on Web sites for Information Professionals which will include a monthly column, weekly research tip, and newsletters. Librarians already know how powerful they are — and how valuable the information they champion is. Therefore, they should be provided the training, tools, and support they need to make sure everyone else in their organization knows it, too."

Resources should be designed to provide information professionals with the practical tools, examples, and templates needed to develop the skills and competencies which will help 21st Century Librarians to thrive.

Since librarians are ultimately responsible for marketing themselves and library services, then the schools that prepare future librarians must offer necessary training to equip them. Library schools should not emphasis only on the skills and knowledge that a librarian needs to do the job but also on how to market to a constituency. Marketing should be embedded in the curriculum as part of other courses by all Library Schools. Training of tomorrow's Information Professionals must start today. The concept of marketing should be widely discussed and accepted professionally and this acceptance has to find its way into library schools' curricula.

It is time to focus on the profession and the professional. No big company should think that it does not need the services of a librarian. A library without a librarian is nothing more than a document storage facility. With or without walls, librarians are masters of information retrieval, management, and delivery. Nobody does it better, and that is the message that current customers, prospective customers, and all humanity should hear. For feasibility of library rebranding, there should be joint efforts coming from library associations, academic institutions, the information industry, and from within the library community.

In the words of Williams (2015), we need to rebrand the library by redefining our relevance in the modern information landscape. He gave some ideas that can help libraries to do this.

Information Science: are we really information specialists?
Many librarians have qualifications in "Library and Information Science", some have "Master of Library and Information Management" however the information management aspect of our profession is one that rarely comes into

discussions. We all talk about research strategies, accessing information, analyzing information, synthesizing information and communicating our new understandings which are definitely fundamental to what we teach as librarians but information science is far more than that. If we truly are information specialists then we need to prove it by being active in our communities beyond lessons on Google search strategies and build our expertise in the rapidly changing global information landscape. As information specialists, we should be on the cutting edge of developments in information science. An example is the concept of "Participatory Culture" described by Henry Jenkins . The key feature of participatory culture is that information is not static; it is a flow of ideas where the modern learner is expected to participate in the dialogue around that knowledge, critique it, share it and collaborate to build new knowledge. Wikipedia is a powerful example in its contrast to print encyclopaedias. An outcome of this for librarians could be that rather than educating students about how to access and use information found on Wikipedia, we teach them how to become Wikipedia editors and participate constructively in this forum.

Approaches to Learning: the library is not just about "research" or "information literacy"

A common narrative in the school setting is this. Students pulsate along in their classes with the usual progression through the curriculum then a unit of study comes up when the students are required to do some research. This becomes the time that they head off to the library and maybe have a lesson on search strategies to get them going in their research. There is nothing wrong with this however pigeon holing the role of the library as the place solely for "research" is unbalanced and greatly limits the role of the library. The library must be seen as a place where all aspects of the Approaches to Learning are inspired in new ways.

For example:

Communication: as information specialists, librarians should enable access to new ways for students to share their learning (e.g. by editing a Wikipedia article) or helping them to understand the conventions of various online forums/formats (e.g. gaming sites).

Collaboration: as information specialists we can collaborate with students to find new ways to work effectively with others beyond the walls of our schools.

Organization skills: as information specialists we can collaborate with students in their inquiries to enable them to organize their data collection and presentations

Affective skills: through flexible scheduling libraries can provide a valuable space and time within the busy school environment for students to self regulate and manage their many demands. The library has a vital role in providing a supportive learning environment.

Reflection: The library is a public space – the entire school community (parents, students, teachers and visitors) all pass through the library at one time or another. This means the library is an ideal place for students to display their learning allowing them to reflect on their process and the summative elements while the school community as a whole has the opportunity to reflect on the learning that is happening across the continuum.

Information literacy skills: the library needs to move beyond one dimensional conception.

Critical thinking: the library is a place of providence and discovery, where the shelves represent a collection of ideas and inspirations from all over the world. The library is therefore an ideal space to challenge thinking, find contrary arguments, challenge assumptions and discover new perspectives.

Creative-thinking: creativity does not happen in a vacuum of thought generation. Creativity is the process of taking what we know and imagining a new unforeseen reality. What we know can be challenged and expanded by digging into the multidisciplinary space of the library where ideas and inspirations from all corners of the planet (and beyond) can provide the trigger for new imaginings.

Transfer skills: students should enable to connect their learning and skills across disciplines. As a prominent public space, the library provides an ideal setting for this transfer of skills.

These are just a few basic examples that demonstrate the need for libraries to represent far more than information literacy.

Future libraries need to be defined by some key concepts.
Many, if not most, of the traditional roles of the library in the education setting remain strong, relevant and powerful however how these roles are reflected in our spaces and practice needs to change. Future libraries need key concepts to guide the decisions we make now that will have a profound impact on the role of our libraries in the future. Student learning must be number one. I know this sounds obvious but in practice, during meetings it is

often an element that gets buried under administrative needs or egos. With student learning at the centre, here are a few concepts to make a start:

Student agency: a focus on enabling a sense of ownership and autonomy that sees the students empowered to access, inhabit, collaborate and leave the library as they need to. Our physical infrastructure (e.g. self checkout counters), our administration processes, our curriculum integration and our resources must be in the service of building student agency.

Responsive: our teaching and our spaces must be differentiated in response to diversity in our school community. There is little excuse in the modern environment for resource acquisition not to be responsive and nimble. Our resources should be able to respond in a timely manner to the needs of our students. No more static stacks of print or outdated databases. Our print and electronic resources should be nimble and relevant.

Flexible and adaptive: static schedules, rigid lesson structures and predefined procedures need to give way to processes and teaching that allow us to meet the needs of our students. A basic detail could be shelving on wheels, furniture that can be readily reconfigured by the students, library bookings that change from week to week, and a librarian who can always be interrupted.

These are just a start but they are fundamental if a library is to remain progressive, relevant and future proof.

Back to Rebranding Libraries

As a result, the rebranding of our libraries comes not in the trusted name of the "library" but in the evolution of traditional practices into new and dynamic approaches that then come to define what the "library" represents in a community (Williams, 2015).

The world of information is changing with each passing day. As information professionals we must adjust or we will cease to be relevant. We should be proactive and adopt rebranding as a survival strategy. We should be brave enough to face our new roles as information specialists. We also have to face the challenges that will confront us and overcome them.

Challenges to be likely faced in an attempt to rebrand

There are numerous challenges that information specialists must deal with. In many libraries and information centres in the developing world like Nigeria, there are the challenges of hardware and software, connectivity/cost, infrastructure and furniture, epileptic power supply and professional expertise.

Lack of expertise:

The pressure that a knowledge society exerts on information specialists hinders their efforts to rebrand library services. The information specialists may lack expertise to maintain the appropriate hardware and software for ensuring that rebranding flourishes. There is great expense involved in recruiting experts to teach or give advice on, say, using library management software to carry out retrospective cataloguing and classification.

Connectivity:
Another challenge is that of connectivity. Service providers are the key to Internet connectivity. But in most developing countries like Nigeria there is low bandwidth. This causes failures in the downloading of online-based resources such as e-books and e-journals that are in high demand because of their currency. Hence there is slow progress in digitizing university libraries and information specialists could therefore fail in their efforts to satisfy customers' expectations.

Epileptic power supply:

Power cuts are negatively affecting the development of IT technology in developing countries. Epileptic power supply affect Internet access, but most libraries and other institutions such as museums and archive centres are automated with all their services offered on-line. Power outages contribute to system breakdowns and poor service, leaving the users deploring the services offered by information specialists.

Lack of Infrastructure

Another glaring challenge is the lack of infrastructure and furniture to accommodate the computer technology needed to service the growing needs of users who want to be part of the knowledge society so that they access a variety of on-line databases, journals and other resources that offer up to date information. Information specialists find themselves handicapped when seeking to deliver good service.

Thus the above challenges have greatly impacted on information specialists' attempts to bring about a new look to the service that they provide in the library.

CHAPTER 9
BUSINESS PLAN

Having a concrete business plan and updating it on a regular basis gives an entrepreneur a blueprint for success. Good businesses always keep their Plan up to date. If you are serious about business, taking planning seriously is critical to your success.

A business plan is a formal written document containing business goals, the methods on how these goals can be attained, and the time frame within which these goals need to be achieved. Wikipedia

In its simplest form, a business plan is a guide—a roadmap for your business that outlines goals and details how you plan to achieve those goals. Planning _By: Tim Berry

If you have ever scribbled a business idea on a piece of paper with a few tasks to accomplish, you have written a business plan—or at least the very basic components of one. At its heart, a business plan is just a plan for how your business is going to work, and how you are going to make it succeed.

A business plan goes on forever, meaning that you are constantly fine-tuning or amending it, because you are regularly evaluating your business health, so the printed version is like a picture of what the plan was on the day that it was printed.

In all cases, the most important element of business planning is the review schedule. Set specific times to review your progress towards your goals. Your business plan review can be done once in a month or quarterly. It is worthy to note that it is the time to review your progress on milestones and to compare your actuals against your financial projections. A real business plan is always wrong—hence the regular review and revisions—and never done, because the process of review and revising is vital.

How should you present your business plan?

A business plan should only become printed document on select occasions, like when you need to share information with outsiders or team members. Otherwise, it should be dynamic document that you maintain on your computer.

Reasons for a business plan:

- To test the feasibility of your business idea by performing market research
- To describe how you will market your products and services to customers
- To obtain financing or attract investors
- To forecast future expansion such as acquiring new equipment, hiring employees or subcontractors, etc

A formal business plan document includes elements like:

- An executive summary
- A company overview
- Some information about your products and/or services
- Your marketing plan
- A list of major company milestones
- Some information about each member of the management team and their role in the company
- Details of your company's financial plan

Who needs a business plan?

When business plan is mentioned, what comes to mind of some people is starting a new business or applying for business loans but it is far more than that. Business plans are also very important for running a business whether or not it needs new loans or new investments. Existing businesses should have business plans that they maintain and update as market conditions change and as new opportunities arise.

Every business has long-term and short-term goals, sales targets, and expense budgets—a business plan encompasses all of those things and is as useful to a startup trying to raise funds as it is to an old business that wants to keep growing.

If you are just planning on picking up some temporary job to supplement your income, you can hop the business plan. But, if you are embarking on a major endeavor that is likely to take a lot of time, money, and resources, then you need   a   business   plan.

1. Startup businesses

A typical business planning set-up is for a startup, the plan helps the founders break uncertainties down into meaningful pieces, like the sales projection, expense budget, milestones, and tasks.

The need becomes obvious as soon as an entrepreneur (Librarian) realizes that he or she does not know how much money needed, and when it is needed, without laying out projected sales, costs, expenses, and timing of payments. This is for all startups, whether or not they need to convince investors, banks, or friends and family to release their money and fund the new venture. In this case, the business plan focuses on explaining what the new company is going to do, how it is going to accomplish its goals, and stating why the founders are the right people to do the job. A startup business plan gives in detail the amount of money needed to get the business off the ground, and through the initial growth phases that will hopefully lead to profitability.

2. Existing businesses

Business plans can be a critical driver of growth for existing businesses. Existing businesses need business plan to set the schedule for regular review and revision.

They use business plans to strategically manage and steer the business, not just to address changes in their markets and to take advantage of new opportunities. They use a plan to reinforce strategy, establish metrics, manage responsibilities and goals, track results, and manage and plan resources including critical cash flow.

For existing businesses, a robust business planning process can be a competitive advantage that drives faster growth and greater innovation.

Instead of a static document, business plans in existing businesses become dynamic tools that are used to track growth and spot potential problems before they derail the business.

Choosing the right kind of business plan for your business

Business plans serve many different purposes and they come in many different forms depending on the audience and the type of business. Plans can also differ greatly in presentation length, and detail. This means that you need to know who your audience are and also put into consideration the goals you want to achieve. Components such as sales forecasts and marketing strategy are found in almost every business plan.

For example, if you are building a plan for an academic library, your plan will go into details about the university approval processes. If you are writing a plan for a cybercafé, details about location and maintenance might be critical factors. And, the language you would use in the cybercafé business plan would be much more technical than the language you would use in the plan for academic library.

Plans that are used exclusively for internal strategic planning and management might use more casual language and this kind of plan never leave the office. On the other, a plan that is destined for the desk of a top venture capitalist will have a high degree of polish and will focus on the high-growth aspects of the business and the experienced team that is going to deliver eye-catching results.

Some common types of business plans by Kateri Kosta

One-page business plan
A one-page business plan is exactly what it sounds like: a quick summary of your business delivered on a single page. This does not mean a very small font size and cramming tons of information onto a single page—it means that the business is described in very concise language that is direct and to-the-point.

A one-page business plan can serve two purposes. First, it can be a great tool to introduce the business to outsiders, such as potential investors. Since investors have very little time to read detailed business plans, a simple one-page plan is often a better approach to get that first meeting. Later in the process, a more detailed plan will be needed, but the one-page plan is great for getting in the door.

This simple plan format is also great for early-stage companies that just want to sketch out their idea in broad strokes. Think of the one-page business plan as an expanded version of jotting your idea down on a napkin. Keeping the business idea on one page makes it easy to see the entire concept at a glance and quickly refine concepts as new ideas come up.

The Lean Business Plan

A Lean Plan is more detailed than a one-page plan and includes more financial information, but it is not as long as traditional business plan. Lean Plans are more likely to be used internally as tools for strategic planning and growth.

The Lean Business Plan dispenses with the formalities that are needed when presenting a plan externally for a loan or investment and focuses almost exclusively on business strategy, tactics, milestones, metrics, budgets, and forecasts.

These lean business plans skip sections like company history and management team since everyone in the company almost certainly knows this information. You do not do an exit strategy section of your business plan if you are not writing for investors and therefore you are not concerned with an exit.

The simplest lean business plan uses bullet points to define strategy, tactics, concrete specific dates and tasks, and essential numbers including projected sales, spending, and cash flow. It is just five to 10 pages when printed. And few Lean Plans need printing. Leave them on the computer. Review and revise them at least once a month. The first Lean Plan takes just a few hours to do (or less), and a monthly review and revision can take only an hour or two per month.

Lean business plans are management tools used to guide the growth of both startups and existing businesses. They help business owners think through strategic decisions and measure progress towards goals.

External business plan (a.k.a the standard business plan document)

External business plans, the formal business plan documents, are designed to be read by outsiders to provide information about a business. The most common use of a full business plan is to convince investors to fund a business, and the second most common is to support a loan application. Occasionally this type of business plan is also used to recruit or train or absorb key employees, but that is much less common.

A formal business plan document is an extension of the internal business plan or the Lean Plan. It's mostly a snapshot of the internal plan as it existed at a certain time. But while an internal plan is short on polish and formality, a formal business plan document should be very well-presented, with more attention to detail in the language and format.

In addition, an external plan details how potential funds are going to be used. Investors do not just hand over cash with no strings attached—they want to understand how their funds will be used and what the expected return on their investment is.

Finally, external plans put a strong emphasis on the team that is building the company. Investors invest in people rather than ideas, so it's critical to include biographies of key team members and how their background and experience is going   to   help   grow   the   company.

Elements of formal business plan

It is noteworthy that in discussion of several different types of business plans, there are key components that appear in virtually all business plans. These elements include the milestones, review schedule, responsibilities, metrics (numerical goals that can be tracked), strategy summary and basic projections. The projections include sales, costs, expenses, and cash flow.

These core elements grow naturally as needed by the business for the actual business purpose.

Executive summary

First impression matters a lot, the executive summary is your business's front desk officer. It needs to be snappy and go straight to the key highlights of the plan. Some potential investors may never make it further than the executive summary, so it needs to be convincing and captivating.

The executive summary should provide a quick overview of the problem your business solves, your solution to the problem, the business's target market, key financial highlights, and a summary of who does what on the management team.

While it is difficult to convey everything you might want to convey in the executive summary, keeping it short is critical. If you hook your reader, they will find more detail in the body of the plan as they continue reading. You could consider using your one-page business plan as your executive summary.

The opportunity

One often useful section of a formal plan describes the market, including market analysis, data, projections, descriptions, and competition.

Target market

As your company is solving a problem that people or other businesses have, it is equally important to specify who you are selling to. Understanding your target market is a key to building marketing campaigns and sales processes that work. Your target market determines how your company grows.

Market trends

Explain the current happenings in your target market and explain how those trends will favour your products or services over those of your competitors.

Market growth

A growing market is encouraging since it suggests a stronger demand for your solution in the years to come. Under here, research is the key. Explain how your target market has been growing or shrinking in recent years. You can use Internet searches, trade associations, market research firms, journalists who cover your market, or other credible sources to measure market growth.

Competition

What other options do your customers have to address their needs, and what makes your solution better for them?

Execution

Products and services

The products and services section of your business plan delves into the core of what you are trying to achieve. In this section, you will detail the problem you are solving, how you are solving it, the competitive landscape, and your business's competitive edge.

Depending on the type of company you are starting, this section may also detail the technologies you are using, intellectual property that you own, and other key factors about the products that you are building now and plan on building in the future.

Marketing and sales

The marketing and sales plan details the strategies that you will use to reach your target market. This portion of your business plan provides an overview of how you will position your company in the market, how you will price your products and services, how you will promote your offerings, and any sales processes you need to have in place.

Operations

Depending on the specifics of your business, include plans related to locations and facilities, technology, and regulatory issues.

Milestones and metrics

Plans are nothing without solid implementation. The milestones and metrics chapter of your business plan lays out concrete tasks that you plan to accomplish, complete with due dates, and the names of the people to be held responsible.

This chapter should also detail the key metrics that you plan to use to track the growth of your business. This could include the number of sales leads generated, the number of page views to your web site, or any other critical metric that helps determine the health of your business.

Company overview

For external plans, the company overview is a brief summary of the company's legal structure, ownership, history, and location. It is common to include a mission statement in the company overview, but that is certainly not a critical component of all business plans. The company overview is often omitted from internal plans.

Team

The management team chapter of a business plan is mainly for entrepreneurs seeking investment but can be omitted for virtually any other type of business plan.

The management team section should include relevant team bios that explain why your management personnel are made up of the right people for the roles. it is a talented entrepreneur who can take those ideas and turn them into thriving businesses.

Business plans should help identify not only the strengths of a business, but areas that need improvement and gaps that need to be filled. Identifying gaps in the management team shows knowledge and foresight, not a lack of ability to build the business.

Financial plan

The financial plan is a vital component of nearly all business plans. Running a successful business means paying close attention to how much money you are bringing in, and how much money you are spending. A good financial plan helps determining when to increase staff strength or procure a new piece of equipment.

A solid financial plan helps a startup that is seeking funding, to figure out how much capital the business needs to get started or to grow, so as to know how much money to ask for from the bank or from investors. A typical financial plan includes: Sales forecast Personnel plan Profit and loss statement Cash flow statement Balance sheet.

How to write a business plan use sample plans

Looking at examples can help you see in your mind's eye what a full, traditional plan looks like, so you know what you are aiming at before you get started. The following are simple steps to be taken:

1. Get a sample plan from a similar type of business

An entrepreneur (librarian) that wants to draw a business plan does not necessarily need to get a business plan that is an exact fit for his or her business. The business location, target market, and even the particular product or service may not match exactly to the plans on ground. You do not need an exact match for it to be helpful. Just look for a plan that is related to the type of business you are starting.

For instance, if you want to start a bookshop, a plan for a business centre (Xerox) can be a great match. While the specifics of your actual startup will differ, the elements you would want to include in your bookshop business plan are likely to be very similar.

2. Use a sample as a guide

If you want your plan to be a useful tool for starting a business—and getting funding if you need it, then avoid copying a sample plan word for word (do not be a copycat). It just will not be as helpful, since each business is unique. Let the business plan sample serve as a guide.

When you go through the process of writing a business plan by yourself, then you will enjoy the benefits that are attached to self written business plan. When you sit down to write, you will naturally think through important pieces, like your startup costs, your target market, and any market analysis or research you will need to do to be successful.

Everyone has competition you will therefore look at where you stand among your competition and lay out your goals and the milestones you will need to meet. Looking at financial section of a sample plan can be helpful because you can see what should be included, but don not presume that financial projections for a sample company will fit your own small business.

3. Think of business planning as a process, instead of a document

Do not see a business plan as a document you create once and never look at again rather think about it as something you do often. If you take the time to write a plan that really fits your own company, it will be a better, more useful tool to grow your business. It will make it easier to share your vision and strategy to your team members making everyone on your team to be on the same page.

4. Fine-tune your plan on a regular basis to use it as a business management tool

Keep in mind that businesses that use their plan as a management tool to help run their business grow faster than those businesses that do not. For that to be true for your company, you will think of part of your business planning process as tracking your actual results against your financial forecast on a regular basis.

When your business is going well, your plan will help you think about how you can re-invest in your business. If you find that you are not meeting goals, you might need to adjust your budgets or your sales forecast. Either way, tracking your progress compared to your plan can help you adjust quickly when you identify challenges and opportunities— this is one of the most powerful things you can do to grow your business.

In a nutshell, an entrepreneur that has a business plan will definitely do better than the one that does not have any pan. Taking the simple step forward to do any planning at all will certainly put your business at a significant advantage over businesses that just drive forward with no specific plans. Although, writing a business plan does not guarantee your success but the best way of getting value from your business plan is to use it as an ongoing management tool. To do this, your business plan must be constantly revisited and revised to reflect current conditions and the new information that you have collected as you run your day to day business activities.

You learn new things every day when you are running a business. Your business plan should be a reflection of those new things you learned to guide your future strategy.

Chapter 10

SWOT ANALYSIS

Information Technology has created a new gateway for information services. Information products and services in a multiple format have made libraries and information centers more competitive and they are now at alert. Libraries are being subject to significant pressure from the information revolution. The rapid growth of materials, increased user based, networking demands competition by database vendors and complexity in information requirements are forcing professionals to seek for various ways of improving the management of the library and information centers in order to remain modern and relevant.

Marketing of library products and making sure that these products get to the end users at the right time and in a good shape through the right channels are part of the objectives of library and information centers. One of the ways of making these happen is by adoption of SWOT analysis into the system.

SWOT is the acronym for Strengths, Weaknesses, Opportunities, and Threats. It is a structured planning method used to evaluate the strengths, weaknesses, opportunities, and threats involved in a project or in a business. A SWOT analysis is designed to provide information that shows a company the best way to use its resources and capability in its business. Also, the purpose of a SWOT analysis is to use those facts, which shows a picture of where your business stands right now, so your team can discuss.

You may think that you already know everything that you need to do to succeed in achieving your organizational set goals but SWOT analysis is a tool for auditing an organization and its environment. It is the first stage of planning and helps organization to focus on key factors. When you take time to do a SWOT analysis, you will be armed with a solid strategy for prioritizing the work that you need to do to grow your business.

A SWOT analysis is a very simple, yet powerful tool to help you develop your business strategy, whether you are building a startup or guiding an existing company. A SWOT analysis helps you understand internal and external factors that can make or mar your success toward your organizational goal. The SWOT analysis process is a brainstorming technique.

It organizes your top strengths, weaknesses, opportunities, and threats into an organized list; it is usually presented in a simple two-by-two grid. Examples of SWOT analysis in marketing include competitors, prices of raw materials, and customer shopping trends.

Strengths and weaknesses are internal to your company, they are things that you have some control over and can change. Examples include who is on your team, your patents and intellectual property, and your location. A SWOT analysis will force you to look at your business in new ways and from new directions. You will look at your strengths and weaknesses, and how you can leverage those to take advantage of the opportunities and threats that exist in your market.

A business can use a SWOT analysis to assess its place in the market. The SWOT Analysis tool is used to objectively analyze a company and understand what it needs to do in order to improve on its performance in the marketplace. Strengths and weaknesses, opportunities and threats may seem obvious and straightforward ways to assess a business.

Opportunities: these refer to positive and favorable external factors that could give an organization a competitive advantage. For example, if a country reduces tariffs, a manufacturer can export its products into a new market which will in turn lead to increased sales and market share.

Opportunities are a combination of different external circumstances at a given time that offer a positive outcome, if taken advantage of. They are things that are happening outside your company, in the larger market. You can take advantage of opportunities and guard against threats, but you cannot change them. Examples include competitors, prices of raw materials, and customer shopping trends. It can also be seen from other light that opportunities are external factors that allow an organization to take advantages of the organizational strength, overcome organizational weaknesses and reduce the effect of environmental threat.

SWOT analysis helps you to build on what you do well, to address what you are lacking, to minimize risks, and to take the greatest possible advantage of chances for success.
SWOT analysis focuses on all different aspects of an organization; it can help with quick decision making and also helps in strategizing: to determine threats which need to be acted on.

THREATS

In business analysis, threats are anything that could cause damage to your organization, venture, or product. This could include natural disasters, anything from other companies who might intrude on your market, supply shortages which might prevent you from manufacturing a product etc. Threats are negative and external condition that can cause an organization a serious damage, hindrances and change in the marketing environment. Sometimes, threat can be so over whelming that the company will have little or nothing to do in savaging the situation. Any external occurrence or event that is worrisome which prevents an organization from either achieving set goals, or taking advantage of presented opportunities can said to be a threat. In a nut shell, threats refer to those external factors that one does not have control over which have the potential to harm an organization.

STRENGTH

Strength is an internal factor that helps an organization to achieve its set goals. Strength is something that gives an organization an edge over others. For instance, your greatest strength happens to be a skill you need in doing a job. Your greatest strength sets you apart from other candidates (to be outstanding). Also, a librarian displays his capability when he is able to solve information needs of a library clientele. As a librarian, you show off your communication skills when you provide answers to questions. Gruel and TAT (2017) see organizational strength as those competencies that help an organization in achieving its set goals.

WEAKNESS

Weaknesses can refer to those internal factors such as low quality of products and services which can hinder an organization from accomplishing its set goals. In the words of Thompson and Strickland (1989), "a weakness is something an organization lacks or does poorly in comparison to others or a condition that puts it at a disadvantage". Such weaknesses may range from insufficient research and development facilities, unskilled manpower, depreciating machinery, poor decision making, narrow product range etc. It is worthy to note that the above mentioned weaknesses can be controlled if guarded against and improved on.

Examples of the best weaknesses to mention in an interview:

1. I focus too much on the details.
2. I have a hard time letting go of a project.
3. I have trouble saying "no."
4. I get impatient when projects run beyond the deadline.
5. I could use more experience.
6. I sometimes lack confidence.

How can you turn your weaknesses into strengths?

1. Recognize and accept your weaknesses.
2. Get guidance from someone you trust.
3. Be very prepared.
4. Hire the skills you lack.
5. Get just good enough.
6. Look for ways to serve others that have the same problem.

How do you turn opportunities into strengths?
The **SWOT/TOWS** (threats, opportunities, weaknesses, strengths) model helps groups develop a prioritized set of strategies and next actions to leverage their strengths and opportunities, and minimize weaknesses and threats. This is a collaborative, reusable model that can be used in strategy development. Within the workplace, the best way to capitalize on your strengths is to use

them. When a problem arises, put your skills to work. Suggest methods of problem solving that you can contribute to.

Examples of SWOT Threats

- Competition: The potential actions of a competitor are the most common type of threat in a business context.
- Talent: Loss of talent or an inability to recruit talent.
- Market Entry: The potential for new competitors to enter your market.
- Customer Service.
- Quality.
- Knowledge.
- Customer Perceptions.
- Customer Needs.

Some examples of strengths include:

- Enthusiasm.
- Trustworthiness.
- Creativity.
- Discipline.
- Patience.
- Respectfulness.
- Determination.
- Dedication.

How to use SWOT analysis to formulate strategies

1. Strengths–Opportunities. Use your internal strengths to take advantage of opportunities.

2. Strengths-Threats. Use your strengths to minimize threats.
3. Weaknesses-Opportunities. Improve weaknesses by taking advantage of opportunities.
4. Weaknesses-Threats. Work to eliminate weaknesses to avoid threats.

SWOT analysis help in the strategic marketing process in some ways for instance, A SWOT Analysis is used to develop strategies that capitalize on an organization's strengths, minimize the effects of any weaknesses, exploit available opportunities and defend against threats. Implementing these strategies leads to achieving the organization's objectives.

Things you need to do before conducting a SWOT analysis.

1. Decide on the objective of your SWOT analysis.
2. Research your business, industry and market.
3. List your business's strengths.
4. List your business's weaknesses.
5. List potential opportunities for your business.
6. List potential threats to your business.

The information needed for a SWOT analysis comes from internal and external sources, including financial resources, market surveys, performance indicators and competitor performance statistics.

Who should do a SWOT analysis?

For a SWOT analysis to be effective, all hands must be on deck. Company founders and leaders (stakeholders) need to be deeply involved. This is not a task that can be delegated to just subordinate though, company leadership should not do the work on their own either. For best results, you will want to gather a group of people who have different perspectives on the company. Select people who can represent different units of your organization, from circulation unit to readers' service unit to reference unit etc. Everyone should have a seat at the table.

Library as service delivery organization can even look outside its own internal ranks when doing a SWOT analysis and get input from customers to add their unique voice to the mix.

If you are starting or running a business on your own, you can still do a SWOT analysis. Take on additional points of view from friends who know a little about your business, your vendors and even suppliers. The essence is to have different points of view or opinion.

Existing businesses can use a SWOT analysis to appraise their current state of affairs and agree on a strategy to move forward. But, remember that things are constantly changing and you will want to reassess your strategy, starting with a new SWOT analysis every six to twelve months.

For startups, a SWOT analysis is part of the business planning process. It will help arrange a plan so that you start off on the right foot and know the direction that you plan on going.

The right way of doing a SWOT analysis

Like earlier stated, you want to gather a team of people together to work on a SWOT analysis. You do not need an all-day activity to get it done, though. One or two hours should be more than enough.

Gather people from different units of the library and make sure that you have representatives from every unit. You will find that different groups within the library will have entirely different perspectives that will be critical to making your SWOT analysis successful.

Doing a SWOT analysis is similar to brainstorming meetings, and there are right and wrong ways to run them. It is advisable to give everyone a pad of sticky-notes and have everyone quietly generate ideas on their own to start things off. This prevents groupthink and ensures that all voices are heard.

After five to ten minutes of private brainstorming, put all the sticky-notes up on the wall and group similar ideas together. Allow anyone to add additional notes at this point if someone else's idea sparks a new thought.

Once all of the ideas are organized, it is time to rank the ideas. You should have a prioritized list of ideas. Of course, the list is now up for discussion and debate, and someone in the room should be able to make the final call on the priority.

You need to follow this process of generating ideas for each of the four quadrants of your SWOT analysis: Strengths, Weaknesses, Opportunities, and Threats.

Questions that can help stir your analysis

Here are a few questions that you can ask your team when you are building your SWOT analysis. These questions can help explain each section and ignite creative thinking.

Strengths: Strengths are things that are within your control. They are internal, positive attributes of your company. Answers to the following questions will help an organization strategize better.

- What business processes are successful?
- What assets do you have in your team, such as knowledge, education, network, skills, and reputation?
- What physical assets do you have, such as customers, equipment, technology, cash, and patents?
- What competitive advantages do you have over your competition?

Weaknesses: Weaknesses are things that you might need to improve on to be competitive. They are negative factors that reduce quality or value from your strengths. Answers to the following questions will help an organization to be on a look out for such factors and also look for a way of reducing its effects.

- Are there things that your business needs to be competitive?
- What business processes need improvement?

- Are there tangible assets that your company needs, such as money or equipment?
- Are there gaps on your team?
- Is your location ideal for your success?

Opportunities: These are external factors in your business environment that are likely to contribute to your success when managed well. Answers to these questions will lead to increased production and effective service delivery

- Is your market growing and are there trends that will encourage people to buy more of what you are selling?
- Are there upcoming events that your company may be able to take advantage of to grow the business?
- Are there upcoming changes to regulations that might impact your company positively?
- If your business is up and running, do customers think highly of you?

Threats: Threats are external factors that you have no control over. You may want to consider putting in place contingency plans for dealing with them should they occur. Answers to the following questions will help you to strategize and be on a lookout.

- Do you have potential competitors who may enter your market?

- Will suppliers always be able to supply the raw materials you need at the prices you need and at the right time?

- Could future developments in technology change how you do business?

- Is consumer behavior changing in a way that could negatively impact your business?

- Are there market trends that could become a threat?

Through the fore going, there is no gainsay that SWOT analysis is a roadmap for gathering **information** that can be fine-tuned with input from internal and external factors.

Disadvantages of SWOT Analysis

1. SWOT analysis is only one stage of business planning

SWOT analysis is one of the components of business planning. It is therefore not advisable for an organization to completely depend on SWOT analysis for business planning because it requires several pieces of data, research, and analysis. You may rather make it a major contributor to your planning depending on your topic.

For you to make appropriate and intelligent decisions and for your business to grow and be profitable, you need more than a SWOT analysis. To achieve this, you will want as much information as possible through other means. SWOT analysis will give you just an aspect of research on four primary functions.

2. A lack of hierarchy leads to problems

SWOT is a study of four categories and these four categories are the only points included in the analysis. If it does not fit into one of these four: Strengths, Weaknesses, Opportunities and threat, it is pushed aside.

The problem lies in the lack of hierarchy. Which section needs your attention first? Which one needs it the least? Only you can decide because SWOT analysis does not say. If you decide wrongly on which one to come first, that could jeopardize your success in the future. Since there is no hierarchy of needs in SWOT analysis, you may not be able to see where your time is most needed and this is a danger signal to a business.

3. Too much structure leads to poor decision-making

In SWOT analysis, you are expected to categorize attributes in only one of the four categories. You can not overlap. Meaning, once something is defined as a weakness, it cannot ever be placed in the other three categories. Strength is strength, never a weakness. An opportunity can never be a threat.

Such a rigid approach will lead to problems. The real world does not follow strict rules or guidance. A person can be charismatic but also a negative character. A business can have unending customers, yet still be in a financial mess. Nothing is ever just *one* thing flexibility is a key to business breakthrough.

4. SWOT analysis becomes impossibly subjective without the right information

Basically, strategic business decisions should be based on reliable and relevant information. SWOT analysis goes against the format of using facts and data from reputable sources. Unlike other formal analyses, SWOT doesn't require scholarly information to be successful. In 10 minutes, you can start and finish your analysis. Regardless of time, people recommend brainstorming throughout the SWOT analysis process. Unfortunately, doing this makes it more prone to bias. Without formal data, the only thing a person can use is their own opinion. Whether that is true or not affects the integrity of the analysis. Not only that, but the information can also become outdated within a matter of hours.

5. Information overload affects your results

As earlier stated most people sit down and brainstorm during their SWOT analysis. No idea is too small or dumb to be added. You can add it as a bullet-list or expand each point until your fingers cramp. Although this can be a selling point for the analysis, it is also a hindrance. Before long, you will have a ton of information on your hands. And not all of it may be usable.

As you now know, SWOT analysis does not tell you where to focus your efforts. It also does not have a threshold for information. You will never know if you have too much or too little. Although that can be a problem, the real issue lies elsewhere. Specifically, you may have too much information for a section that does not matter as much as another.

For example: You will likely stray closer to the threats section if you are planning for risks. Strengths are not a necessity here. Neither are opportunities. But weaknesses which can turn into threats needs focus too. You may run into issues if you spent more time discussing strengths and opportunities than threats and weaknesses. With too little information in the latter sections, your risk planning analysis will be incomplete.

Chapter 11

Entrepreneurship education

We live in a world where the future is uncertain, and it belongs to creators and innovators. And that is why it is important to learn and study **entrepreneurship**. Entrepreneurship education serves as an excellent foundation for the types of creative, innovative ideas we need to succeed in the 21st century. Udeh (1999) states that "an education that does not result in the ability to create ideas and transform the ideas into physical realities is not a true education" In a nutshell, Education – enlightenment – Identification – Result

The world has never been more in need of students who are trying to make a difference than it is today. And this is the very definition of entrepreneurs. Their goal is just to sell products and services in a profitable way. To become successful at it, they have to identify the real needs and problems of people and find a way of solving them. Even fresh out of the entrepreneurship education program, the students have this unique mindset of finding problems that need to be solved, invent a solution for them, and, ultimately, make the world a better place.

Fayolle and Gailly (2004) defined entrepreneurship education as any pedagogical programme, associated with inculcating entrepreneurial skills and qualities in learners. Similarly, Oduwaiye (2009) described entrepreneurship education as the scope of lectures, curricular and programmes that attempt to provide students with the necessary entrepreneurial competencies, knowledge and skills, geared towards the pursuit of a career in entrepreneurship. In nutshell, entrepreneurship education, main goal is to inculcate entrepreneurial skills in learners which will in turn culminate in entrepreneurial behaviour and action.

Education is the process of acquiring knowledge, special skills and experiences by an individual for effective conquering and adaptation to his environment. Entrepreneurship education seeks to provide students with the knowledge, skills and motivation to encourage entrepreneurial success in a variety of settings. Variations of entrepreneurial education are offered at all levels of schooling from primary or secondary schools through graduate university programs . The entrepreneurship can provide new division and it can make good students for world (Wikipedia, 2012).

Entrepreneurship training is designed to teach one the skills and knowledge that is needed before embarking on a new business venture. Though the programme may not assure one of being successful, but it equips trainees with the rudiment of entrepreneurship which will guide them in avoiding many of the pitfalls awaiting less trained colleagues.

The objectives of entrepreneurship education according to Mbiewa (2011) include: to provide graduates with necessary skills that will make them to be creative. Provide small and medium size companies with the opportunity to recruit graduates who possess relevant skills to manage business enterprises

Standard education programs ranging from secondary to high institutions are optimized to reflect the "education for everyone" campaign. While the idea behind this movement is great and essentially good, it does not mean that it brings out the best in the students. Many students float away from their talents because they are allowed to answer to their callings rather they are pushed to study medicine, law, maths and their likes.

Entrepreneurship education is a lifelong learning process, starting as early as elementary school and progressing through all levels of education, including

adult education. The entrepreneur is always learning and developing appropriate competence by solving problems of the business as they arise, an entrepreneur will always want opportunities to learn and develop the knowledge, skills and attitude that will enhance business performances as well as cope with problems of change.

Learning entrepreneurship is very different from learning anything else. The very concept of the program is to help the students identify their strengths and talents and to work on improving them. In real-world examples, we can see many successful entrepreneurs who were very bad students in their time but succeeded in business. Bill Gates is a college dropout and look at him today the whole world wants to reckon with him because of his success in business. Introducing entrepreneurship into our educational curricular as a subject or a course is a welcome development because it will do us well.

Studying entrepreneurship will benefit students from different social and economic backgrounds because it teaches people to cultivate **unique skills** and think outside the box. It also creates opportunities, instils confidence, ensures and stimulates the economy.

According to Arvanites et al (2009), innovative educational methods are needed to develop the entrepreneurial spirit and talents that are necessary to function effectively in an environment of strong market forces and complex people issues. They added that for entrepreneurship education to be most useful, it must address and develop in students, the skills essential for them to thrive as entrepreneurs.

Entrepreneurship education provides up-and-coming entrepreneurs with the skills and knowledge to come up with business ideas and develop their own ventures. And this includes helping them to learn about core business areas such as sales, marketing, management and finance, among others and broader ranging skills such as adaptability, effective communication, and confidence.

Risk is something to live with, this is another important lesson that entrepreneurship programs teach students. Risk is something natural, something that we have to live with, and something that has to be managed. There is no other school program that teaches this. In fact, to be honest, most of us have been thought throughout our education even at our homes that we need to stay away from risks and that certainty is the best path to take.

In the world of business, risk is a common occurrence. And to be able to succeed in it, you have to work on your character traits – risk-taking and perseverance. An entrepreneurship program fosters these character traits. This is why it is beneficial for students when they find themselves in a real-life situation.

The benefit of learning **entrepreneurial skills** over traditional subjects is that they are not exclusively relevant to **a career as an entrepreneur**. The skills needed to start your own business are relevant in any field and would also be advantageous qualities for being an employee. In fact, having a wide range of business-relevant skills acquired through studying entrepreneurship would make a person an ideal candidate in most fields. Therefore, skills taught in entrepreneurial courses generally apply to all areas of industry and do not kill creativity or block opportunity to a specific career.

The ability to think critically is essential to success in business world. Unfortunately, it is not something that is being encouraged in traditional schools (Arvanite, 2009). Entrepreneurship education stimulates and challenges students into creative and innovative ideas and concepts that result into setting-up and sustaining business ventures and other investment opportunities. Traditional models of education fall short in their ability to link the knowledge and concepts covered in the classrooms to the skills and practice of entrepreneurship. Traditional learning methods most commonly employed in management education provide learning experiences that are inadequate in several respects. Entrepreneurship training is important because, a company is not something bound to run smoothly forever, especially today, when markets are more volatile than ever. Not to mention the harsh competition.

Students have to be exposed to real-world examples and learn from their own experiences. Entrepreneurship education exposes students to numerous opportunities to learn how to think critically and analyze the pieces on the board. Being aware of all the important factors and seeing how they affect each other is the foundation of a smart decision-making process. This is not something that can be learned from a book but through critical thinking.

In addition, strong interpersonal skills such as financial literacy, money management, associated with entrepreneurs, are not only beneficial but also relevant for day-to-day life activities. However, the benefits of entrepreneurship education go beyond being purely personal; they are also beneficial to society at large. The economic benefits of entrepreneurs to society have never been in doubt. New enterprise and entrepreneurial innovation are critical for any society to be globally competitive, with technological advancements creating new jobs.

Entrepreneurship is important as it has the ability to improve standards of living and create wealth, not only for the entrepreneurs, but also for related businesses. Entrepreneurs also help drive change with innovation, where new and improved products enable new markets to be developed

As our education system becomes plagued with rigid testing and standards, opportunities to innovate, collaborate and demonstrate proficiency in real life situations become rare. In addition to encouraging people, entrepreneurship education requires students to be innovative, creative and collaborative with others.

For our society to benefit from **entrepreneurship**, we have to equip ourselves with the training to do so. The personal benefits of
studying entrepreneurship spread far beyond the business world leading to a possibly wealthier livelihood. We as a society should be doing more to help develop our entrepreneurial minds.

In Europe, some institutions of higher learning have made entrepreneurship courses requisites for graduation. Some programs already encourage students to start their own companies as early as the high school while certain schools are working with investors and venture capitalists to fund start-ups. (www.masterstudies.com).

It is no surprise that in Nigeria today, our secondary and tertiary institutions' subjects/courses include what should be the centrepiece of contemporary education: entrepreneurship. Thanks to forward-thinking individuals. Nowadays, studying and learning the art of entrepreneurship is easier thank you think.

Entrepreneurship Education in Nigeria

Nigerian educational system is a colonial heritage and as such, does not have much consideration for entrepreneurship education. The colonial education was designed to assist colonial masters in breaking communication gap between them and Nigerians. Emphasis was placed on producing clerical and administrative officers, teachers, clergy and other liberal arts graduates who would facilitate the westernization process.
The post independence governments did not do much to restructure our education curricular, right from the primary, secondary through the tertiary stage. Liberal arts, through rote learning, dominated our educational system. Akinyemi (1987) notes that our educational institutions, few as they were, remained factories for producing white collar jobbers with no special profession nor was entrepreneurial skills envisaged in the educational system.

The Federal government, being worried by the high level of unemployment, deteriorating per capita income, youths agitation in various parts of the country, directed all tertiary institutions in the country to run entrepreneurship studies programme as a compulsory course for all students irrespective of their disciplines with effect from 2007/2008 academic session Although the Federal Government made entrepreneurship education compulsory, some universities are yet to commence it with a degree of seriousness. By making entrepreneurship studies compulsory, government is aiming at producing opportunity or knowledge-based entrepreneurs who are expected to be critical growth drivers of our economy (Okojie,2009).

From the fore going, it can be deduced that entrepreneurship education is still at infancy in Nigerian universities, the fact remains that one of the policy goals of university education as well-established in the National Policy on Education, is the development of entrepreneurial skills among undergraduates. The essence of it all is for universities in Nigeria to demonstrate entrepreneurial capabilities in their offerings, targeted at training graduates that would be job creators rather than employment seekers.

 It is a thing of joy that government has made entrepreneurship studies compulsory in our tertiary institutions; it is bad news that most of our universities are not yet ready for full implementation. Akinbami (2011) study on entrepreneurship studies in the country's tertiary institutions notes that: Different meanings are ascribed to entrepreneurship education in different tertiary institutions in the country. Some of these programmes commonly present entrepreneurship education programmes in   the   context   of vocational training rather than developing the spirit of entrepreneurship, which is the stimulation of entrepreneurship activities and performances in various disciplines. The country's universities were not prepared for entrepreneurship education when they were compelled to commence it. It is not clear whether any special fund has been made available to the universities for the prosecution of entrepreneurship education. The same conventional facilities for conventional education are being used in the universities. The same personnel for conventional courses are being used for the teaching of entrepreneurial studies in our universities (Akinbami 2011).

Challenges of Entrepreneurship Education in Nigeria

The instruction of Federal Government for immediate introduction of entrepreneurship education in all tertiary institutions in the country has made it a career course in transition. Stakeholders in education have initiated it but the destination is still far going by many challenges facing it. These challenges include, but not limited to the following:

Hasty Preparations: The government's directive for immediate commencement of the programme is appreciated considering its advantages, but preparations before the commencement were hasty. A pilot test using some selected institutions would have gone a long way in preparing and arming them with vital information.

Instructional Materials: Instructional materials are all forms of information carriers that can be used in recording, storing, and transmitting or retrieving information for purposes of teaching and learning. According to Ezike and Obodo (1991) instructional materials are those instruments teachers use in classroom for teaching. Adekola (2010) noted that instructional materials are one of the factors influencing functional education in Nigeria. Regrettably, instructional materials used in teaching entrepreneurship education in Nigeria are not adequate to address modem trends of skill acquisition in the society. There are lacks of quality entrepreneurial textbooks in Nigerian schools even the teaching methods in use does not suit the practical aspect of entrepreneurial education. In line with this, Obeleagu-Nzelibe and Moruku (2010) noted that the state of infrastructure in Nigerian university system is, embarrassing. According to them, Academic Staff Union of Universities (ASSU), has argued in several negotiations with the Federal Government over low infrastructural levels in university system which hinders free flow of activities in the campuses. There is no gainsaying that poor state of infrastructure in Nigerian public universities is not encouraging as the new entrepreneurship education will only worsen the situation.

In competency of Teachers: Institutions in Nigeria do not have adequate and high level manpower for effective teaching and learning of entrepreneurship education in the country. Entrepreneurial education is expected to prepare learners to be creative and productive citizens and nation builders, therefore; teachers implementing the curriculum in the classroom are supposed to be competent in different skills and delivery methods. A learner can only be creative and productive when guided by experts who possess practical skills. Though there is need for entrepreneurial education, Nigeria is lacking the manpower in the school system that can effectively implement the curricula at various levels of education in the country. The available teachers were drafted from the existing faculties and have not got additional skills to cope with the challenges of the new curriculum. Since one cannot give what one does not have, the expected products of the new entrepreneurship education may not perform any miracles if they are lectured by the same old lecturers.

Poor attitude to technical and vocational education: Entrepreneurial education cut across different technical and vocational areas. Poor societal attitude to vocational and technical education poses a big problem to entrepreneurial education. Despite government efforts in enhancing technical and vocational education, it is still perceived as the form of education for the under-privileged children. Though high level of unemployment together with insecurity should have changed this attitude, but Nigerians still prefer general education.

Inadequate funding: Though the government directed for immediate commencement of entrepreneurship studies in all tertiary institutions, no special funds have been made to the universities despite the new responsibilities. New classroom blocks, workshops, laboratories, books, academic journals, lecturers, computers, among other materials are required for successful implementation of the new programme. (Obeleagu-Nzelibe and Moruku 2010)

STRATEGIES FOR ACHIEVING FUNCTIONAL ENTREPRENEURIAL EDUCATION

According to Ayodele (2006), the disregard of functional entrepreneurial education in Nigeria is rubbing the nation of the contributions these unemployed youths who are now perpetuating evil in the society would make on the economy. Though the nation is suffering many problems but neglect of this aspect of education (entrepreneurship) could be said to be responsible for the increasing rate of insecurity in the country. Youths that should have been utilized as competent bibliographers, indexers, auto mechanics, database technicians, plumbers, electricians, medical technicians etc are now utilizing their creative energy in causing havoc to the society. But all hope is not yet lost as there are different strategies, which could assist in achieving a functional entrepreneurship education in Nigeria. Some of the strategies include:

Incorporation of School-Work Based Learning: Entrepreneurial education differs from other curriculum in that it encompasses an individual's total life style which is relevant to nation building and sustainable security' consequently school-work based learning should be integrated into the entire curriculum from basic school through graduate level rather than viewed as an isolated unit of instruction studied at a particular time and level. According to Ayodele (2006), for functional entrepreneurial education to be achieved, there should be some form of genuine school-work based learning incorporated in some studies as part of the national economic development strategies.

Adequate Funding: Availability of fund in every educational program is a critical factor in achieving functionality of such program. The unavailability of fund to our schools makes the cry for entrepreneurial education to be on papers than practices. Well funded entrepreneurial education program will no doubt equip the schools with adequate facilities needed for efficiency of the subject and achieving the stipulated objectives of entrepreneurial education thereby eradicating insurgence of insecurity. Government alone cannot fund functional entrepreneurial education as it demand for incorporation of different experts from varying skills.

Provision of modern, relevant and adequate facilities for entrepreneurship training will result in having products who will not be the same dysfunctional job seekers as has been hitherto the case. If relevant training facilities with the right personnel are provided, the products of the system will be the envisaged creative and innovative job makers.

Therefore, both public and private funds should be pooled to finance the high cost of inviting skilled craftsperson into formal teaching process.

Introduction of Entrepreneurship Education at Primary and Secondary Level: Introducing entrepreneurial activities to students at early ages will help in building a solid foundation before university education. This will make it all embracing, procedural and comprehensive for the desired solid foundation at the university level. When products of primary and secondary education come to the university they are better prepared for a functional entrepreneurship university education

Development of Internship Programs: Skills learning is more of practical than theory; students from time to time should be matched with local successful entrepreneurs with sound educational background who will mentor them. To enhance economic efficiency, self-empowerment and acquisition of useful skills, learners should be made to pass through an expert who will mentor them under the supervision of the school. There are many problems in learning vocational skills, which cannot be found in books but through internship programmes, a learner can gain solutions to such problems through the help of an experienced entrepreneur.

Establishment of Vocational Centres: There is need to shift the focus of our education from certificate base to skill oriented. This could be achieved by establishing vocational centres for the youths. School students should be mandated to engage in practical during holidays in such centres with the help of teachers offering supervision services to the centres. In such centres, students should be encouraged to carry out some activities like writing business plan, feasibility study, seek for credit facilities, etc under a typical entrepreneurial condition as in the society. They should be taught how to form cooperative society and start theirs in the centres.

Competency Based Recruitment of Teachers: Functional entrepreneurial education in our schools is expected to produce high quality graduates who are competent in different skills. It is therefore important to consider calibre of teachers that should handle the subject in different levels of education. Assigning of the subject to people who are not vocationally and technically trained is like a blind leading another blind man. Vocational and Technical education which entrepreneurial education is part of should be handled by quality teachers with skill oriented educational background. There is no gainsaying that quality of education provided in any society and nature of change effected is determined by the quality of teachers and the effectiveness of their teaching methods.

Recruitment and assigning of this subject/course to anybody should be based on performance not certificate. To achieve this, interviewers and management should base their judgment on pedagogical skills, occupational skills, knowledge and attitudinal competencies needed for effective teaching of entrepreneurship in schools.

Entrepreneurship education is very vital for entrepreneurship expansion because it is the engine that propels creativity and innovations into practical manifestations in form of business ventures and other investment opportunities. Without a functional education the manifestation of entrepreneurship skills in individuals may be difficult.
It not wrong to say that the people behind businesses are entrepreneurs and they can best perform if they adopt best practices which entrepreneurship education can offer.

Entrepreneurial opportunities for LIS graduates

Recognition of opportunity is the beginning of entrepreneurial activity. However, opportunity can be looked for or created by individual.
There are many career opportunities available to library and information science professionals all over the world. The challenge is for them to be able to identify and recognize entrepreneurial opportunities and fully exploit them.

Opportunity refers to the possibility of putting available or existing resources to good use in order to achieve given ends. They are positive external options that an individual could exploit to accomplish a mission, goals or objectives. It can therefore be said that an opportunity is a recognized need in the market place to which an entrepreneur has a response or solution to.
Akanwa, Anyanwu & Ossai-Onah (2014) define entrepreneurial opportunities as set of business ideas or conditions that are open for exploitation when perceived. Entrepreneurial opportunity exists whenever there is a need, want, problem or challenges that can be addressed, solved and or satisfied in an innovative way.

Entrepreneurial opportunities can be seen as purposive situations that necessitate the discovery of means and contact through which new goods, services, raw materials, and organizing technique can be introduced to bring into being economic value. They are eye-catching investment ideas, scheme that provides the possibility of an gainful return for the investor or the person taking the risks. They lead to the provision of products and services that create or add value for its consumer.

Types of Entrepreneurial Opportunities

Entrepreneurial opportunities can be categorized into two, namely: innovative opportunities and exploitative opportunities.

i.   **Innovative Opportunities:** Here, the innovator is absolutely in charge of this opportunity in which case, only those with innovative ability can maximize such opportunities by virtue of their innovative insight. The fact is that the innovation observes the existence of opportunity. It is a process of creating new, I profitable products and ideas by incorporating observations or insights taken from elsewhere into the work one had previously being doing. Innovation is. I defined as the generation and introduction of new ideas, which lead to the development of new products and services, processes, and systems in all areas of business activity.

ii.   **Exploitable opportunity (Open opportunity):** This opportunity is opened to anyone who has the capacity of seeing an unexploited market through the information available. In this case, the individual with deep insight with analytical mind can easily manipulate such opportunity for maximum return on investment. These kinds of entrepreneurial opportunity are highly competitive unlike the innovative opportunity.

iii.   Entrepreneurial opportunities in I library and information science profession are different ways to develop new ideas that will improve the state of library and information service. Library and information science practitioners should recognized profitable opportunities and act upon them. In the case of Library and information profession, an entrepreneurial opportunity exists where there is a need, want, problem or challenges in librarianship that can be addressed solved and or satisfied in an innovative way. It is about recognition or discovery of new ways of providing library and information services and allied in information related services. It is note worthy that the integration of information .and communication technologies (ICT) in librarianship has led to the existence of various entrepreneurial opportunities for library and information professional. This kind of business opportunities are referred to as library and information science-based businesses and are as follows:

- Library equipment business
- Publishing and printing business
- Information brokerage business
- Library consultancy business
- Rural information provision business
- Stationary business
- Reprographic business
- Vendor business
- Freelance information business
- Information communication technology-based business among others.

The above are some of the entrepreneurial opportunities in the library and information profession. LIS graduates can venture into any of them and make a fortune. Before any of these business opportunities is ventured into, the entrepreneur needs to have an in-depth understanding of how it operates: what it is all about, its scope, environment, market structure, present status, foreseeable future, sustainability and continuity as a means of income.

There are many business opportunities in library and information services but until they are discovered, they cannot be harnessed. It is therefore left for LIS graduates to discover new opportunities within the landscape of information services. The available opportunities should be seized and properly utilized for business advantages. The windows of opportunities must be properly x-rayed for maximum exploitation. It is worthy to note that one of the keys to maximizing entrepreneurial opportunity is the availability of timely and relevant information. The level of information available to an individual constitutes an entrepreneurial opportunity. Availability of opportunities does not easily transform to reality. Recognition of opportunity is an essential factor in maximizing entrepreneurial opportunities. However, after recognizing an opportunity there is need to understand it and be able to come up with possible means of addressing the problem.

Library and information science graduates must take absolute care in the identification of the products and services wrapped up in the opportunity they want to explore to avoid making costly mistake. It is worthy to note that proper analysis of available opportunities will empower library and information science graduates on the practical steps to take in order to establish small scale business. Taking pragmatic steps to exploit opportunities is determined by the level of the graduates' understanding of the profitable openings. It is not, enough to identify an opportunity, it is imperative that one is fully acquainted with the basic information that will engineer the optimal utilization of recognized openings. It is expected that the resources needed to exploit a business idea or opportunity ought to be perceived ahead and on time. Having seen a list of the various opportunities in library and information science, in the broad terms however, it is very important that library and information science graduates are acquainted with the knowledge of what is required to establish one or more of them.

ICT Businesses

Information and communication technologies have created various business opportunities for individuals especially those that possess the skills. In the words of Emmanuel (2017), Information and communication technology (ICT) has permeated all nooks and crannies of human life, be it education, health, transportation, tourism, trade and commerce, industry and aviation. She defined ICT as "an electronic and communication tool invented by man to assist him in the performance of various tasks which ordinarily were cumbersome, time consuming and complex if carried out manually".

According to Onah, Adebayo and Igwe (2014), ICT is an umbrella term that includes all technologies for the manipulation and communication of information. Thus, ICT encompasses the following:

- any electronic medium to record information (magnetic disk/tape, optical disks, CD, DVD, flash memory, drives etc.);

- technology for broadcasting information - radio, television;

- technology for communicating through voice and sound or images - microphone, camera, loudspeaker, telephone to cellular phones. It includes the wide variety of computing hardware (PCs, servers, mainframes, networked storage), the rapidly developing personal hardware market comprising mobile phones, personal devices, MP3 players, and much more;

- full gamut of application software from the smallest home-developed spreadsheet to the largest enterprise packages and online software services; as well as

- the hardware and software needed to operate networks for transmission of information, again ranging from a home network to the largest global private networks operated by major commercial enterprises and, of course, the Internet.

There are now many viable entrepreneurial opportunities which graduates of LIS can venture into using ICTs. These opportunities can be micro, small or medium scale in nature. ICT Businesses can be defined as buying, selling and servicing of the technologies for human satisfaction. ICT businesses can be successfully operated in urban, semi-urban and rural locations. The businesses are relevant and are required more in environments with large population of individuals such as academic environment.

ICT-Based Businesses cover marketing, sales and services related to ICTs such as computer systems, hardware and software accessories of computers telephones, telephone accessories, audio and audio-visual resources (CD films, movies, CD-ROMs of information resources). It also includes opera cyber cafes, phone call centres, owing a cinema, hiring projectors, rendering video and photo coverage services, and the likes.

(a) Marketing of ICT components: Marketing of ICT components business involves sale of complete computer systems, hardware and software components as well as input and output devices required for the operation of computer systems. Others are complete accessories, scanners, printers, uninterrupted power supply, digital cameras, flash drives, modems, projectors, MP3, anti-vi software, connecting cables, etc.

(b) Sales of Telephones and its accessories: Mobile telephones are now a most to buy by every adult even children. It has now become a necessity and not a luxury as it facilitates easy communication amongst individuals in a society. Sales of telephones accessories are now a booming business here in Nigeria.

© **Servicing of Computer systems and Telephones:** This has to do with repairs and maintenance of computer systems and telephones. Most of these systems are sub standard and as such develop faults easily thereby creating jobs for ICT-based entrepreneur with required skills.

(d) Establishment of ICT Training Centres: ICT training is money making machine. A LIS graduate with a wealth of ITC skill can decide to open a center where individuals can come and acquire computer/ICT skills for manipulation of computer systems and other digital gadgets. The operators of such centre may be rendering executive training services to people in their various homes or offices. They can also collaborate with primary and secondary schools for the provision of ICT skills training to their students at reasonable and subsidized fees. Example of this is the just concluded workshop organized by the Library and Information Science Department, Rivers State University for their students on 11th September 2020 titled 'Digital Skills for Students'.

There is no doubt that graduates of LIS are competent professionals, who possess practical ICT skills and have excellent knowledge of ICT components and accessories. In line with this, Onah, Adebayo and Igwe (2014) noted that ICT-related issues form significant part of LIS curriculum in tertiary institutions. So graduates of LIS that have requisite ICT skills will perform creditably and succeed in ICT businesses.

Contemporarily, all ICT businesses are booming because everyone in the society even a non literate market woman has a need for it and this has given a rise to many prospects in the business. In this era of globalization, individuals and organizations cannot thrive without application and utilization of ICTs. Thus, the ICT businesses contribute positively to the growth and development of man. This is why every serious minded LIS graduate will always be in business he or she will use knowledge of ICT skills to: Access, produce, organize, communicate, create, engage, and program any system.

Freelancing

Freelancing is a contract-based profession where instead of being recruited in an organization, the person uses his skills and experience to provide services to a number of clients. In simple terms, freelancing is when you use your skills, education, and experience to work with multiple clients and take on various assignments without committing to a single employer. The number of assignments or tasks that you can take just boils down to your ability to deliver on them as asked from them.

People who engage in freelance work are called freelancers or freelance specialists. Freelancers earn money by selling their work or services to different organizations rather than being employed by one particular establishment (Hornby, 2010).

Freelancing usually involves jobs (called gigs) that allow you to work-from-home situations. But do not associate freelancing as the same as having a work-from-home job. Freelancing does not always mean that you will work from home. You might have to work at your client's office too depending upon the type of work and the client's requirements. Also, a work from home job involves a contract between you and a single employer who gives you a salary while freelancing does not. It is just that many of the jobs that freelancers perform can be delivered over the Internet without their presence at the company or clients place.

Freelancing takes place in almost all professions. Library and Information Science (LIS) graduate have to engage in certain freelance businesses within the LIS profession. Such LIS-related freelance ventures are referred to as freelance information businesses. The concept called freelance information business is coined to encapsulate information products and services that are amenable to freelance business activities (Ekuoye, 2007 and Igbeka, 2008).

Nnadozie, Okeke and Egwim (2014) defined freelance information business as a situation in which people earn money by doing information-related works or rendering information services without being employed by the recipient individuals or organizations.

What qualifies a person for categorization as a freelance information service provider is the ability to deliver the needed fee-based information service to different individuals and organizations without necessarily being employed as their staff

The nature of LIS curriculum prepares LIS professional to easily fit into and succeed in any information-related ventures. Although the span of freelance information ventures is enormous, the following business activities are specifically recommended to LIS graduate: web administration, content management, document delivery service, information repackaging, digitization of library materials, marketing of library and information service, freelance writing/journalism, copy editing, freelance photography, book reviewing and advertisement agency.

Freelancing has positive as well as negative side. You just have to decide if you are willing to take the risk that almost always accompanies it. Freelancing means professional freedom, but it also means instability and the risk of failure. And that may not be what you need in your professional life. But if you risk your stability for something more in tune with your professional goals than a traditional job, you have the opportunity to build your name and reputation and reach your professional goals.

But if you love the freedom, flexibility, and earning potential that comes with being independent, then freelancing is an ideal situation.

Reprography

Reprography which is also known as reprinting is the reproduction of graphics through mechanical or electrical means, such as photography or xerography. Reprography is commonly used in catalogues and archives, as well as in the architectural, engineering, and construction industries. Wikipedia. Reitz (2004) defines reprography as "a general term encompassing quick-service document reproduction or copying by any means except large scale professional printing, including photography, microphotography, xerography, and photo duplication". Reprography comes in form of photography or xerography. There are diverse types of reprographic reproduction and they include: scanning, photocopies also referred to as xerography, photographs, and digital images. Reprography as a business is not able to operate as a self contained unit; it cannot work without computer network or system.

Typical items produced by reprographers include architectural/engineering blueprints and renderings, indoor and outdoor signage, maps, billboards, backlit displays, trade show graphics, legal and medical exhibits, etc.

Large-format reproductions are produced with a variety of technologies

dependent, in part, on the application of the final product and quantity needed.

Reproductions can be made from the same size or smaller/larger hard copy originals. Prints can also be computer generated from CADD (computer aided design and drafting) files or from a growing variety of desktop publishing and design software packages.

In addition to addressing the large-format reproduction needs of their customers, reprographers frequently sell reprographic equipment and consumable supplies. Other business services such as mounting and lamination, quick copying, microfilming, scanning and facility management may also be provided.

Facsimile Business

Facsimile business is one of the businesses that a LIS graduate can delve into and make a fortune. Facsimile transmission means sending texts or images, over telephone lines, of texts or images printed or handwritten on a sheet of paper to a recipient. These days, fax machines are cheap and very easy to acquire by anyone unlike those days when Fax Machines are being bought as single equipment and mainly owned by communication companies and big organizations. LIS graduates can make money by sending documents via fax to their customers. It is as simple as getting the number of the potential recipient and negotiate the cost for the document transfer. In fax business, both the sender and the recipient need to have a Fax machine and a fax number. The fax machine is equipped with a scanner, a printer and a modem with a dedicated line and fax number. Through facsimile, manuscripts, drawings, graphs, pictures, agreements, building plans, court injunctions, seminar papers, drafts, fliers, invitation cards, wedding cards, calendars, receipts, could be sent and received.

Photocopying Business/Stationery Business

Photocopying in academic environment is a lucrative business this is because everyone in community must have one thing or the other to duplicate. Ritz (2004) sees Photocopying as the act of reproducing graphics by means of passing it through a radiant energy which transfers the content to another medium. This is done by means of photocopier. A photocopier is a machine for making xerographic copies of documents, usually in black and white or coloured.

Stationery Business

Stationery business is a form of business enterprise that has to do with the selling of things used in writing such as paper, envelopes, printed booklets, cash receipt booklets/invoices, wire bound note books, agreement sheets, stamp duty seals, stamps and stamp pads, and their inks of different colours, stencils, carbon papers, cardboard papers, among others to individuals, schools, corporate bodies and the general public at large. It is a form business owned by an individual or a group of persons. According Wikipedia.org, stationery has historically pertained to wide gamut materials: paper and office supplies, writing implements, greeting cards, glue pencil cases and other similar items. The initial capital for stationary business is usually small compare to other businesses. The entrepreneur can be a retailer or wholesaler on it.

The business activities of stationery business further includes: the stocking and sale of photocopier machines, computer sets, printers of various kinds and their cartridges, rewritable and recordable CDs, stabilizers, UPS units, and a host evolving items and gadgets.

The present state of stationery business in Nigeria is quite robust, contrary to expectations that revolution in Information and Communications Technology (ICT) would do away with paper based formats, but in the developing countries like Nigeria the ICT revolution has not affected the use of stationery items in people's daily business because everybody in the society needs one type of stationery item for one reason or the other. Going by the above, there is no gainsaying that stationery business has come to stay and will continue to thrive even in future.

Laminating Business

Lamination business goes hand in hand with photocopying business. It is part of the work done in a place where materials are often used so as to preserve the life of the material by preventing corrosion. Lamination has to do with the covering of a document or book cover with a polythene or water proof, applying pressure or heat in order to prevent it from water, dust or dirt and also to ensure the longevity of such document. Unegbu, (2014) sees lamination as the process of uniting superimposed layers of one or more materials by an adhesive or by other means. It is a bonding of one or more materials into a unit for safety and longevity. Reitz (2004, p.392) defines lamination as "a method of preserving old and fragile documents by adhering a layer of thin transparent plastic film to one or both sides of each sheet by the application of pressure and/or heat, sealing the surface against dust and atmospheric conditions". Lamination entails using a polythene (plastic, water proof) product to protect the material that it covers. Apart from durability, lamination prevents materials from getting soiled with dirty hands and prevents water from damaging them.

Any LIS graduate that involves in lamination business will not lack food to put on his table because lamination materials are very easy to get and secondly, there are many single items to laminate, items such as: Pictures, posters, warnings, directions, catalog tags, shelf tags, art works, plans, drawings, and others. For materials to last long, all the covers must be laminated, covered with plastic materials.

Binding Business

Bookbinding is another lucrative business which LIS graduates can venture into. Every LIS student in the course of their studies during their practical attachment must work in binding unit of any library they choose to do their attachment. In libraries, printing companies, workers are employed solely for binding books. Apart from binding new productions in a book industry or projects in tertiary institutions, deteriorating books are put back to use by rebinding. There is always job available for bookbinders. According to Odiase, Unegbu and Haliso (2001), binding is "part of the book that holds the leaves or pages together. It protects the leaves and makes them easy to handle". In printing, binding is the sewing or stitching of the outside covering of a volume of printed or blank leaves at the spine. Nobody talks of binding without mentioning books, and most of the times we combine book and binding to create the nouns 'bookbinding' and 'bookbinder'. From Wikipedia, the free encyclopedia, Bookbinding is the process of physically assembling a book from a number of folded or unfolded sheets of paper or other materials. It involves attachment of a book cover to the resulting text-block. Bookbinding is a handiwork learned in a school of printing or learned under the tutelage of a workman as an apprentice. But in this modern era, books are bound in mass, so we have mass-produced books by high speed machines in bindery factories as against the hand binding by individuals.

 There are different types of bookbinding. Some are named according to the type of materials used and others according to the type of operation performed. There are hardcover binding and soft cover or paperback binding. Hardcover binding, which is also called hardbound book, involves using rigid cover which is stitched at the spine. Any type of binding that is not hardcover is soft cover irrespective of the method or material used. (Unegbu, 2014 p 285)

For LIS graduate who wants to set up personal business as a reprographer who is wondering an environment where the business will thrive, the business booms in an academic environment mostly in tertiary institutions. Other areas where reprographic business can also thrive are Anywhere that people congregate in large groups on daily basis. Places like court premises for photocopying court decisions, companies for typing and photocopying documents of transactions - receipts, agreements, orders, hospital premises, publishing firms, daily market place etc are good environment reprographic business.

Rural areas are other area for such business. Villagers may have documents to be sent to many individuals or places, they need to photocopy them. They may lack even printer to print the documents or even typist to type them so that becomes a business opportunity for a reprographer.

In the words of Unegbu (2014), as long as human beings continue to exist on the face of the earth, reprographic business will continue to thrive. Hitherto it has been generating employment to thousands of people. Everywhere you go you see reprographic outfits. One good thing about the business is that it does not need large premises to operate neither does it need many and sophisticated equipments. All you need is to erect a good catchy signboard not billboard to showcase what you can do. Comply with the local government's rules and regulations in writing and placing billboards. As long as students bind their projects, theses, dissertations and as long as some of them are lazy as to miss their classes and use their fellow students' note's to copy, this business will continue. The future of this business is very bright. Scanning, which is part of this reprographic business has no foreseeable end. Even overseas universities request for recommendation letters written on letterhead papers scanned and sent to them. (Unegbu, 2014),

Vendor Business

Nigerians are known for hustling and hustling is encouraged in Nigeria. Considering the era we are in, any graduate of LIS who is smart and creative will succeed as a vendor not only in Nigeria but the world at large.

A vendor is a person selling something. An example of a vendor is a man with a stall at a university's gate who is selling books or writing materials. A person or a company can vend or sell. In a clearer way, a vendor or a supplier is an intermediary between a product/services and the recipient.

Vendor business encompasses all the activities relevant to the purchase and stocking of virtual or physical information-bearing materials for sale to libraries, corporate organizations or individuals.

According to Obinyan (2014), One overriding motivation for vendor business in Nigeria is that given the existing promising business terrain, there is hope for anyone who is smart and creative to succeed as a vendor. In Nigeria, there are close to one hundred and fifty registered publishers with many more spread over the nation turning out large books to be read. One of the essential aspects of book publishing and a challenge to publishers is distribution and marketing of books, publishers will eagerly collaborate with any vendor who is interested in the distribution of published outputs. Distribution of information related products and services is one of the focal points of vendor business. Distribution since time immemorial has been known as indomitable impediment to gainful publishing business in Nigeria any vendor that earnestly want to be effective and relevant will make good money.

Vendor is a general term used to refer to a third party, other than a publisher that sells content and supporting services specifically to libraries and related information centres. Most of these vendors have a focus on either books or serials aside from some specialty vendors that distribute and market audiovisual materials. Book vendors interchangeably referred to as booksellers, dealers, or jobbers, now sell book to libraries that a few years ago might have been bought direct from the publishers.

A vendor therefore is a person who supplies materials, inventory, or services needed to support the operation of sustainable vendor businesses while at the same time adding value to the products and services to create wealth. In a more general sense, a vendor is any individual, company or agency that provides information products and/or services to the consumers or those desirous of the products of interest for a fee.

Types of vendors/suppliers

- Service and maintenance providers perform services.
- Manufacturers make goods from raw materials.
- Wholesalers sell goods to other businesses.
- Retailers sell goods to individual consumers.

Skills, Interests and Qualities

To be a vendor, you should have:

- Good customer service skills a smart appearance
- The ability to talk knowledgeably and enthusiastically about books
- Good communication skills
- The ability to sell, promote and market the products
- Self-confidence and optimistic
- Able to take calculated risk
- Energetic and diligent
- Creative, perceptive and resourceful

Sustainability in any business depends on certain factors. For a vendor to ensure continuity in business, he/she must have the interest of the customers at heart. For example the vendor must be certain that the products or services he wants to vend are of high quality in order to make the customers get greater value for their money.

For a LIS graduate that is freshly out of school who has little or no capital, a home based business suggested since the start-up expenses for a home based business may require less capital than the expenses for the purchase or lease of a commercial structure.

Information Brokerage

An information broker is a company which specializes in collecting information about individuals from public records and private sources, including census and change of address records, motor vehicle <u>Wikipedia</u> while Kissel (2003 as cited in Ojo 2012) views an *information broker* as an individual who searches for *information* for clients. *Information brokers* use various resources including the Internet, online services that specialize in databases, public libraries, books and CD-ROMs. They also make telephone calls. Information is not only recorded items of knowledge; it is also the digitized bits of information that could be moved through computers and telephone lines to where it is needed (Levine, 1998)

Information Brokerage is the act of searching for information for those that need it (customers) for a fee. In a nutshell, information brokering is the business of buying and selling of information as a product.

It is believed that information brokering - the business of buying and selling information as a

product has been around for a long time. It can be traced to th*e early history of Gutenberg in* the middle 1400s, in which church and government prerogative, involving the distribution of "origin works of art," gave way to mass Production and the business of book publishing (Levine, 1998). Another school of thought opines: ``information brokering as we now think of it as a business opportunity for the individual information professional was begun by the French in1935.Conversely, followed that the concept came from the Societe Fracaise de Radiophone, an organisation of professionals who created the notion of supplying information over the phone for a fee.`` Information brokering as a profession probably has its roots in the 1960s, when a few

individuals and library organizations realized that computer and photocopier,

announces the significant role to be played by technology in the information

revolution,

and impact on information retrieval. The ability to deliver documents, copies

of

published articles, and similar material to the academic, business and

professional

communities, on demand, presented an opportunity to those with enough

foresight and

entrepreneurial spirit to turn the need into business. As a result, information

brokers provide

their clients with information for a fee. They provide research and other

information

services. In Nigeria, according to Igbeka (2008), their job cannot be

specifically defined

since they perform different functions.

Information Brokerage: Business for LIS Graduates

Analysts indicate that the best information brokers in the field often have a background in library science

Information brokers typically start off working in business administration for companies like law firms, medical research facilities, marketing or public relations firms, or other companies this allow them to utilize research skills.

Over time, information brokers typically start their own business where they will promote their services to business and work for several clients at a time to provide them with research strategic Information brokers are skilled in a variety of areas, particularly forms on research, and have the tools and knowledge needed to find out exactly what a client needs to know for their business.

Types of Information Brokers

The following are identified as two distinct types of Information Brokers:

(i) In-House Information Brokers

These types of information brokers often spring from library automation. They put corporate libraries online to outside database services including commercially available online information databases as well as comprehensive database directories.

(ii) Professional Information Brokers

These can be found in companies that are not large enough to have in house information brokers. These companies perform information search services for clients for fees.

Skills needed to successfully operate Information Brokerage Business include: expertise in researching and accessing public, and in some cases private, information over the Internet through traditional sources such as libraries, microfiche archives, and so on. To update a Website, an individual requires basic Web publishing skills. Communication skills should be concise and descriptive.

The international potential of Information Brokering business is unlimited. where a client may reside does not count so long as you have access to the information they seek, you can e-mail it to them, and this makes the borders of your business purely virtual and governed solely by language.

Information brokers provide, for a fee, information retrieved from publicly accessible data sources, most often online databases. Information brokers also known as independent information specialists; often do much more than gathering of information. In this era, when almost anyone can access huge amounts of data over the Internet, brokers look for a way of surviving and being relevant by providing a number of special services, which includ: writing reports that analyze the data they obtain, creating internal databases for clients to manage their in-house information, maintaining current awareness services that update a client whenever new information on a given topic becomes available among others.

From time immemorial, services offered by librarians have been for free this brought about information brokerage. The inspiration behind information brokerage business is about obtaining a fee for professional services, otherwise seen as selling information. Information brokers have an array of business ventures that could engage them in the performance of their information brokerage business.

According to Igbeka (2008), the following are some aspects of the work information brokers are doing in Nigeria:

- Indexing;
- Abstracting;
- Retrospective conversation;
- Cataloguing and Classification (Contract cataloguing);
- Literature reviews;
- Online literature search;
- Print searches for users;
- Owning a library or bookshop with the cooperation of nearby libraries in the area of interlibrary loan;
- Packaging information;
- Editing and publishing;
- Developing hyper media –products;
- Translation;
- Marketing management of library;
- Organization of seminars, conferences, and workshops;
- Presentations (e.g. Microsoft Power Point);
- Creating databases and website design.

A good broker can save a client time and money. While it may be tempting to try to jump on the Internet and do the research yourself (especially for a small businessperson with limited financial resources), searching for data can be an strenuous and time-consuming process, especially if you are not an expert in the area of online searching. In addition, most brokers subscribe to online databases that are not available to the public, even on the Internet.

The future of information brokerage business is bright and promising. As entrepreneurial activity, information brokering is a popular new field that is attracting a lot of attention. Information explosion is paving way for information brokering profession. The more people recognize the vast amount of information available to them, the more they will seek for the assistance of online researchers to efficiently compile that information for them.

Library Equipment Business

High rate of unemployment in the society has made graduates to start looking for ways to adapt and face the challenges that come with it. Library and information profession is a noble profession which equips its graduates with entrepreneurial skills and career options that will make them become employed and also employers of labour. One of the career options is the production, sale and repairs of all kinds of library equipment known as Library equipment business. Library equipment business is a vital and rich avenue where numerous opportunities in librarianship can be fruitfully exploited to provide employment for graduates of library and information sciences and also to make the graduates employers of labour.

Library equipment business will thrive in tertiary institutions because there is always great demand for library equipment by these institutions especially during accreditation exercise. Also, most private schools in the country now know the need for establishment of libraries in their schools. With this development, library equipment will be needed by these schools to enable them set up their school libraries. Library equipment business though capital intensive is very lucrative if managed well by professionals.

Library equipment business is a business covering the production, sale and repairs of library equipment for display, processing and keeping of library information materials for effective service delivery. In producing the equipment, the library and information graduate will apply the expertise knowledge of the profession in designing the equipment. In the production process, the entrepreneur can hire the services of artisans in the area of welding and woodwork to produce samples of the product which he/she will use to advertise for his business.

The business needs full attention of the entrepreneur and for that; he should not be far whenever the equipment are being constructed. The business requires metal and wooden materials as the case may be and therefore requires carefulness so that materials and effort put will not be a waste.

Library equipment includes:
- Metal and wooden shelves, trolley,
- Metal library ladder,- circulation counter,
- Study carrels of different types,
- Metal and wooden newspaper/magazines rack,
- Conference tables,
- Catalogue cabinets
- Book display racks,
- Metal round stool,

- Issuing trays,
- Pigeon holed cupboards,
- Book pockets,
- Book cards,
- Filing cabinet, and
- Others, as may be requested by the customer.

The target customers for the library equipment business include all the heads to both private and public primary and secondary schools In the area of your business location and environments; all the heads of libraries in different institutions of higher learning in your business locality; public institutions such as hospitals; and, all government ministries and parastatals that have departmental libraries. The entrepreneur should equally source for customers in other available information centres.

Like earlier stated, library equipment business is capital intensive and as such a startup entrepreneur will need money for the following basics:
- Warehouse,
- Van,
- Tools,
- Registration of business among
  others.

Since Library equipment business is not like some other ones that entrepreneurs can startup with little or no fund, it is advisable for LIS students to start saving some money even from school or during their youth service year. If the entrepreneur does not have enough money to startup a business, he can use the method of subletting contract to another person for a period of time. In this case, he will do the bidding and tender the limitation, but when the contract is awarded, he gives it to another who will do it and thus parts away with a percentage of the money as shall be agreed. Through this method, the entrepreneur can raise enough money to startup his own Library equipment business someday.

BIBLIOGRAPHY

Akanwa, P.C., Anyanwu, E. U. & Ossai-Onah, O. V. (2014) Entrepreneurial opportunities for LIS graduates. In A. O. Issa, C. P. Uzuegbu & M. C. Nwosu (Eds). Entrepreneurship Studies and Practices in Library and Information Science. Lagos: Waltodany Visual Concept. pp191-197

Acs, Z.J., &Audretsch, D.B. (1988), "Innovation in large and small firms: An empirical analysis", American Economic Review, 78,678-690.

Aderibigbe, O,A. and Farouk, B. L. (2017). *Challenges on marketing of information resources and services in Federal University Libraries in North-West zone of Nigeria.* International Journal of Academic libraries and information science. 5(3), 92 — 96.

Adesanya, O. (2002). *The impact of information technology on information dissemination.* In Everest C. Madu and Marie B. Dirisu (eds) information science and Technology for library schools in African. Evi-Coleman Publication, Ibadan.

Akanwa, P. C. & Udo-Anyanwu, A. J. (2017). *Information resources in libraries.* Owerri: Supreme Publishers.

Akinbami, C.A.[2011] 'Preliminary Issues in Entrepreneurship Education Development- Nigeria   Context.' Ile- Ife, Centre For Industrial Ressearch and Development, Obafemi Awolowo University.

Akinola, A. O. (2013). Entrepreneurship in Nigeria-funding and financing strategies.European Journal of Accounting Auditing and Finance Research, 1 (4), 115-128.

Alsever, J.(2016), Fortune magazine, The Kindle Effect, Retrieved 04/04/2020

ALTER, A. (2016). *"Meredith Wild, a Self-Publisher Making an Imprint". NYT. Retrieved* 04/042020

Alvarez, S. A., & Busenitz, L. W. (*2001*). The entrepreneurship of resource-based theory. Journal of Management, 27(6), 755–775. https:// https://doi.org/10.1177/ retrieved on 17/04/2020 from https://www.google.com/search?q=alvarez+and+Busenitz+2001&rlz= 1C1CHBD_enNG870NG870&oq=alvarez+and+Busenitz+2001&aqs

Amara, T., Ojukwu, K., Okpata, F. & Njoku, R. (2011). *Entrepreneurship* *development.*Aba, Nigeria: Ker Expert Books.

Anderson, A., &Miller, C. (2003), "Class matters: human and social capital in the entrepreneurial process", The Journal of Socio-Economics, 32, 17-36.

Anyanwu, F.A. (2010). *Practice of Entrepreneurship and youth empowerment.*Owerri, Nigeria: Uzopietro

Ardito, S. C. (2003) "Information Brokers and Cyberstalking." *Information Today.*

Baddeley, A. *(2013) "Reedsy could offer self-published authors a professional edge". Retrieved* 08/04/ 2020.

Barnier, O. (2020) financial assets, **https://www.investopedia.com/terms/f/financialasset.asp**

Baskerville, R.F. (2003), "Hofstede Never Studied Culture", Accounting, Organizations and Society, 28(1), 1-14.

Becker, (1975), "Human Capital. Chicago", IL: Chicago University Press.

Begley, T.M., & Boyd, D.P. (1987), "Psychological characteristics associated with performance in entrepreneurial firms and smaller businesses", Journal of Business Venturing, 2, 79-93

Berry, T. (2017) https://articles.bplans.com/author/tim-berry/

Blanchflower, D., Oswald, A., & Stutzer, A. (2001), "Latent entrepreneurship across nations?" European Economic Review, 45,680-691.

Bonnett, C & Furnham, A. (1991), "Who wants to be an entrepreneur? A study of Adolescents interested in a Young Enterprise scheme", Journal of Economic Psychology 12,465-78. 233,509-520. online retrieved on 08/04/2020

Brockhaus, R.H. (1980), "Risk taking propensity of entrepreneurs", Academy of Management Journal,

Building a business as a solopreneur (2017) online retrieved on 16/06/2020 from https://smallbiztrend.com/2017/08/solopreneur-business-ideas.html

Clausen, T.H. (2006), "Who identifies and Exploits entrepreneurial opportunities", online retrieved on 17/04/2020 from www.ccsr.ac.uk

Davis, J. (2015) "Capital Markets and Job Creation in the 21st Century." Washington, DC. https://www.brookings.edu/wp-content/uploads/2016/07/capital_markets.pdf

De Aze, E. E. (2002). *Marketing concepts for libraries and information services. London: Library Association.* http://www.envisionit.com.au/Docs/gandhi.htm>, Accessed on: 4-01-2020.

Drucker, P. F. (1985). *The Practice of Management, London: Heinemann Ltd. Drucker, P. F. (1985).Innovation and entrepreneurship: Practices and principles, New York: Flarper & Row Publishers.*

Eke-Okpala, H. N. and Ihejirika, K. T. (2012) Proposing adoption of entrepreneurial skills for enhanced library practice in Nigeria PAPER · JANUARY 2012 online retrieved on 05/07/2020 http://www.researchgate.net/publication/282507074

Ekuoye, O. (2007). Choosing an area of interest in library and information science. Benin, Nigeria: Justice Jeco Publishers Ltd.

Elonye, G.U. & Uzuegbu, C. P. (2013). Entrepreneurial opportunities for library and information science professionals in contemporary society. The Research Librarian, 7, 23-42

Emmanuel, V. O. (2017). Influence of Information and Communication Technology on Information Dissemination in Libraries of Federal Universities in South South Nigeria: A Dissertation Presented to the Department Library and Information Science, Faculty of Education, Imo State University, Owerri in Partial Fulfillment of the Requirements for the Award of Doctor of Philosophy (Ph.D.) in Library and Information Science.

Enikanselu, S.A. (2008). The complete entrepreneur: Managing the small industry. Lagos, Nigeria: Enykon Consult.

Entrepreneurship education (2019) online, retrieved on 19/07/2020 from https://en.wikipedia.org/wiki/Entrepreneurship_education

European Commission (2010) "Directive of the European Parliament and of the Council". https://www.goodfinancialcents.com/best-business-credit-cards/

Fayolle, A., & Gailly, B. (2004) .Using the Theory of Planned Behaviour to assess Entrepreneurship Teaching Program: A First Experimentation. Paper presented at 14th Annual International Entrepreneurship Conference, Universoty of Napoli federicoii, Italy

Friedman, J. (2017), <u>The Key Book Publishing Paths: 2017</u>, Retrieved 04/04/2020.

Frue, K.(2018)5 Surprising Disadvantages of SWOT Analysis Online retrieved on 24/08/2020 from https://pestleanalysis.com/5-surprising-disadvantages-of-swot-

Gruber, M. (2004) what is a Sales Representative? Online, retrieved on 20/05/2020 from

Gruel, E. &TAT, M. (2017). SWOT analysis: A theoretical review. The Journal of International Social Research, 10(51), 1-13.

Haye, A. (2020). Entrepreneurs Help Economies. Online retrieved on 04/04/2020 from https://www.investopedia.com/terms/e/entrepreneur.asp#entrepreneurs-help-economies

Hiltzik M. (2017). "No, ebooks aren't dying – but their quest to dominate the reading world has hit a speed bump". Chicago Tribune. Retrieved 09/04/2020.

Ho, T.S. & Koh, H.C. (1992), "Differences in psychological characteristics between entrepreneurially inclined and non-entrepreneurially inclined accounting graduates in Singapore", Entrepreneurship, Innovation and Change: An International Journal, 1, 43-54. online retrieved on 08/04/2020

Holt, D.H. (2011). *Entrepreneurship: New venture creation.*New Delhi, PHI learning Private.

Hornby, A. S. (2010). *Oxford advanced learners dictionary.* Oxford: Oxford University Press.

https://globaljournals.org/GJMBR_Volume12/2-Information-Brokerage-an-Entrepreneurial.pdf

https://www.careerexplorer.com/careers/sales-representative/

https://www.thebalanesmb.com/business-marketing-strategies-2948337

Hurst, E., & Lusardi, A. (2004). Liquidity constraints, household *www.scirp.org* › reference › ReferencesPapers online retrieved on 17/04/2020 from

https://www.google.com/search?q=hurst+and+lusardi+2004+article&r
lz=1C1CHBD_enNG870NG870&oq=hurst+and+lusardi+2004+articl

Hutchinson, A. (2019). Library Entrepreneurship: Taking a Lesson from
Business History https://libraryconnect.elsevier.com/articles/library-
entrepreneurship-taking-lesson-business- history

Igbeka, J. U. (2008). *Entrepreneurship in library and information service*
Ibadan, Nigeria: Stirling-Horden Press Ltd.
Igbeka, J.U. (2008). *Entrepreneurship in Library and Information Services.*
Ibadan: Stirling- Horden Publishers Ltd.

Igbeka, J.U. (2008) Entrepreneurship in Library and Information Services.
Ibadan: Stirling-Horden Publishers Ltd. 1-57.

Iwhiwho. E. B. (2006). Information repackaging and libraries services: A
challenge to information professionals in Nigeria. Department of
Library and Information science, Delta State University, Abraka.

Iwhiwhu, B. E. And Okorodudu, P. O. (2012) Public Library Information
Resources,   Facilities, And Services: User Satisfaction With The Edo
State Central Library, Benin-City, Nigeria: Library Philosophy And
Practice (e- journal). Online Retrieved On 19/10/2020 Fro
https://digitalcommons.unl.edu/libphilprac/747/

Jelusic, S. (2003),Publishing And Librarianship In Central And Eastern
Europe: The Needs To Join Forces online retrieve on 04/04/2020 from
https://journals.sagepub.com/doi/abs/10.1177/095574900301500105
Kenton, W. (2020) Understanding Intraprenneurship online retrieved on
17/04/2020
fromhttps://www.investopedia.com/terms/i/intrapreneurship.asp

Kirzner, I.M. (1973). Competition and Entrepreneurship.Chicago, IL:
University of Chicago

Knight, F.H. (1921). Risk, uncertainty, and profit, Library of Economics and
        Liberty. Retrieved on 04/04/2020 from
        www.econlib.org/library/Knight/knRUP1.html
Kollatz. H.J. *(2017). "Self-Publishing". Richmond Magazine.
        Retrieved 08/04/ 2020.*
Kosta, K. (2017) https://articles.bplans.com/author/kateri-kosta/

Kuratko, D. F. & Hodgetts, R. M. (2007).*Entrepreneurship: Theory, process,
        practice* (7th ed.). Mason, OH: Thomson/SouthWestern Publishing

Lake, L. (2019) online retrieved on 04/04/2020 from
Landstrom, H. (1998).The roots of entrepreneurship research. *Lyon, France:
        Oxford*
 Lazarus, S. (2017). "MBO Partners' Latest Report on U.S. Freelance
        Economy Shows a Wage 'Barbell Effect'". Spend Matters.
        Retrieved on 16/06/2020.

Levine, M.M. (1998). "A Brief History of Information Brokering." United
        States of America. Association of Independent Information
        Professional Inc. http://www.aiip.org Accessed 20th April 2011.

Liles, P. R. (1974). New business ventures and the entrepreneur. *Homewood,
        IL:Irwin.*
Linton, I. *(*2019) What Is Publishing? The Seven Processes of Book
        Publishing. Retrieved on 08/04/2020
        fromhttps.//selpublishingadvice.org/7-process-of-
        publishing/view_comments

List of Strength & Weaknesses for Job Interviews Online retrieved on
        24/08/2020 from https://www.monster.com › greatest-strengths-and-
        weaknesses

Madhusudhan, M. (2008). Marketing of Library and Information Services
        and Products in University Libraries: A Case Study of Goa University
        Library. *Library Philosophy and Practice (e-journal).* 175.
        https://digitalcommons.unl.edu/libphilprac/175.

Management History. 12, 9-24.

McClelland, D. C. (1965).Toward a theory of motive acquisition. *American Psychologist,20,* 321-333.

Murphy, J.P, Liao, J & Welsch, P.H. (2006), "A Conceptual history of entrepreneurial thought", Journal of

Nnadozie, C. O., Okeke, I. E. & Egwim, F. O. (2014) Freelance Information Business. In A. O. Issa, C. P. Uzuegbu & M. C. Nwosu (Eds). Entrepreneurship Studies and Practices in Library and Information Science. Lagos : Waltodany Visual Concept. pp.309-317.

Nwachukwu, A. C (2009). The role of entrepreneurship in economic development: The Nigerian perspective. European Journal of Business Management, 4(8).

Nwosu, M. C. (2014), Introduction to Entrepreneurship in A. O. Isa, C. P. Uzuegbu, M. C. Nwosu (Eds,). Entrepreneurship Studies and Practices in Library and Information Science. Umuahia: Zeh Communication. Pp. 3-43

Obeleagu-Nzeribe, C.G. and Moruku, R.K.[2010] ' Entrepreneurship and Economic Development: The Imperative For Curriculum Innovation in Nigeria,' in Mainoma et.al [eds] Conference Proceedings, Faculty of Administration, Nasarawa State University, Keffi, vol.1

Obinyan, G. A. (2014). Vendor Business. In A. O. Issa, C. P. Uzuegbu & M. C. Nwosu (Eds). Entrepreneurship Studies and Practices in Library and Information Science. Lagos: Waltodany Visual Concept. pp277-290

Oduwaiye, R.O. (2009). Entrepreneurship Education in Nigerian Universities: Implementation and Way Forward. Advances in Management, 8(1): 60–67.

Ojo, J. O. (2012). Information brokerage: An entrepreneurial approach to information services in Nigeria. *Global Journal of Management and*Business Research, 12. Online, retrieved on 10/10/2020 fromhttps://globaljournals.org/.../2-Information-Brokerage-an-Entrepreneuria.

Okojie, J.A.[2009]' Imperative of the Federal Government Directive On The Establishment of Entrepreneurship Studies in Nigerian Universities,' A Paper Presented at the 1st Conference on Effective Implementation of Federal Government Seven-Point Agenda Held at NUC, Abuja, Feb.4-6

Olokundun, M A. (2006) Pecerptions Of Students On Entrepreneurship Education And Entrepreneurial Intentions In Selected Nigerian Universities online retrieve on 06/10/2020 http://eprints.covenantuniversity.edu.ng/9506/1/Ayodele.pdf

Onah, E. A, Adebayo, O. A. & Igwe, K. N. (2014). ICT Businesses and Other Viable Entrepreneurial Opportunities Beyond Library and Information Science In A. O. Issa, C. P. Uzuegbu & M. C. Nwosu (Eds). Entrepreneurship Studies and Practices in Library and Information Science. Lagos: Waltodany Visual Concept. pp.319-328

online retrieved on 04/06/2020 from https://www.entrepreneur.com/article/284402

Orna, R. (2019). Retrieved on 04/04/2020 from Https.//selfpublishingadvice.org/category/production-distribution-advice/

Pinki, A. (2013). Entrepreneurship development: Converting dreams into reality. Journal of Business Management & Social Sciences Research (JBM&SSR) 2, *(9).* Online Retrieved 18/04/2020fromhttp://www.zadcomputcrs.co.in/Zad/MDU/StudvMaterial/MBA/Entrepreneurial%20Development.pdf

P r o f e s s i o n a l i s m (2014). Online, Retrieved on 10/10/2020 from http://hosting.caes.uga.edu/2008csrees/pdfs/s54-w

Project Writers Ng (2016), online retrieved on 20/09/2020 from https://www.projectwriters.ng/challenges- of-entrepreneurship-education-in-nigeria/#respond

Rauch, A., & Frese, M. (2000), "Psychological approaches to entrepreneurial success: A general model and an overview of findings", In: Cooper C L, Robertson I T (eds.), International Review of Industrial and Organisational Psychology, 10, 1-41 online retrieved on 08/04/2020

Reitz, J. M. (2004). Photocopying, lamination. In Dictionary for library and information *science* (pp.392, 534). Westport, Connecticut: Libraries Unlimited.

Retirement Plans for Self Employed People". Internal Revenue Service online retrieved on 16/06/2020 from https://www.irs.gov/retirement-plans.for-self-employed-people

Reynolds, P. (1991). Predicting new firm births: Interactions of organizational and human populations. In Sexton, D. L. , & Karsarda online retrieved on 17/04/2020 from https://www.google.com/search?q=Reynolds+1991+work+on+entrepreneur&rlz=1C1CHBD_enNG870NG870&oq=Reynolds+1991+wor

Ricardo, D. (1817). On the Principles of Political Economy and Taxation. London: John Murray.

Riyazuddin. (2012). Marketing of information products and services in some select NGO *Libraries of Delhi and NCR in the areas of health education and women studies.* Retrieved from Home/General/Marketing of Information Products and Services in Library on 12/1/2020.

Robert, D. H. (1986*).Entrepreneurship and intrapreneurship. Lexington, MA: Lexington Books.*

Robinson, P.B., Huefner, J.C., &Hunt, H.K. (1991b), "Entrepreneurial research on student subjects do not generalize to real world entrepreneurs", Journal of Small Business Management, 29, 42-50. Psychological Monographs, 80, Whole No.609 online retrieved on 08/04/2020

Rotter, J. (1966), "Generalised expectancies for internal versus external control reinforcements",

Rotter, J. B. (1966): Social Learning Theory & Locus of Control online retrieved on 04/04/2020 from *https://study.com/academy/lesson/julian-b-rotter-social-learning-theory-locus-of-control.html*

Rowley, J. (2006) *Information Marketing* (2nd ed.). London: Ashgate. Yahaya, O. A. and Wesley, O. (2017): *Information Repackaging: A Panacea for Libraries and Information Resources centres in Nigeria.* International Journal of business and management invention; 6(6) 59-

Say, J. (1834). *A treatise on political economy. Philadelphia: Claxton, Remsen and Haffelfinger.*

Schumpeter, J.A. (1934).The Theory of Economic Development. Cambridge, MA: Harvard University Press

Shamel, C. L. (2002) Building a Brand: Got Librarian? Online retrieved on
07/07/2020 from http://www.infototaday.com/searcher/default.htm

Simpeh, K. N. (2011), entrepreneurship theories and Empirical Research:
Summary Review of the Literature, European Journal of Business and
Management ISSN 2222-2839 (Online) www.iiste.org
Sivakumar, B. (2019) What Is Freelancing? How to Become a Freelancer? –
The Actionable Guide online retrieved on 05/10/2020 from
https://nations1099.com/gig-economy-data-freelancer-study/

*Steve Henn (2014). "Self-Published Authors Make A Living – And
Sometimes A Fortune". NPR. Retrieved 09 2020.Five years ago,
printing your own book was stigmatized and was seen as a mark of
failure...*
Strategies That Capitalize On An Organizations Strengths Marketing. Online
retrieved on 24/08/2020 from https://www.ukessays.com › essays ›
strategies-that-capitalize-on.

SWOT Analysis: How To Conduct Your Marketing SWOT. Online retrieved
on 24/08/2020 from https://www coschedule.com › marketing-strategy
› swot-analysis

Thompson, A. A. & Strickland, A. J. (1989). Strategy Formulation. 4th ed.
USA: Irwin.

Torren, M. (2010). 5 Essential Skills for Entrepreneurial Survival. Retrieved
from http://www.blogtrepreneur.com/2010/09/17/5-essential-skills-
for-entrepreneurialsurvival/

Turning Your SWOT Analysis into Actionable Strategies - Bplans Blog
Online retrieved on 24/08/2020 from https://www
articles.bplans.com › swot-analysis-challenge-day-5-turni...

Udeh, J. O. (1999) Entrepreneurship in the 21st Century: A Training Guide
on Entrepreneurship Studies for Small and Medium-scale Enterprise
Development and Management. CIDJAP Publication

Unegbu, V.E. (2014) Reprographic and Allied Business. In A. O. Issa, C. P.
Uzuegbu & M. C. Nwosu (Eds). Entrepreneurship Studies and
Practices in Library and Information Science. Lagos: Waltodany

Visual Concept. pp299-308

*UNIDO. (1999).Policy benchmarking in the developing countries and the economies in transition: Principles and practices. Retrieved from: www.unido.org/.../32894_*

United States Small Business Profile, *2018" (PDF)*. Small Business Administration. Small Business Administration. online retrieved on 16/06/2020

Utsch, A., Rauch, A., Rothfuss, R., & Frese, M. (1999), "Who becomes a small scale entrepreneur in a post-socialist environment: On the differences between entrepreneurs and managers in East Germany", Journal of Small Business Management 37(3), 31-41 online retrieved on 04/04/2020

Vaishnavi, N. (2017) online, retrieved on 20/05/2020 from https://www.businessmanagementideas.com/marketing/channels/middl eman-meaning-importance-and-functions-distribution-channel/11949

Venkataraman, S. (2000). The distinctive domain of entrepreneurship research: An editor's perspective. In J. Katz, & R. Brockhaus (Eds.), *Advances in entrepreneurship, firm emergence, and growth, 3 (119-138). Greenwich, CT: JAI Press.*

Ward, S. (2019) Advantages of being self employed online retrieved on 16/06/2020 from https://www.thebalancesmb.com/the-advantaes-of-being-a-contractor-2-948558

Wikipedia (2020). Meaning, Importance & Qualities of Packaging online retrieved on 19/14/2020 from www.yourarticlelibrary.com › packaging-and-branding

Wikipedia (2014). S t a t i o n e r y . Retrieved frombftp://en. wikipedia.org/wiki/statione
https://en.wikipedia.org/wiki/Reprography retrieved on 14 August 2020

Williams, P. J. (2015) Rebranding Libraries. Online retrieved on 02/08/2020 from https://thelibraryelement.com/2015/10/24/branding-libraries/#comments

www.ingramcontent.com/pod-product-compliance
Lightning Source LLC
Chambersburg PA
CBHW080925260726
48661CB00010B/3809